Praise for *On a*

"Ziolkowski's descriptions of his waterborne existence are thrilling in their beauty. . . . Whether or not you've ever been on a surfboard, this funny and poignant story opens the heart to the sublime thrill of perfect swells and reminds us of the pain and delight of youthful passion, best friends and first kisses."
—Pat MacEnulty, *Ft. Lauderdale Sun-Sentinel*

"A wistful, elegiac remembrance of a surfing adolescence mingled with a search for life's authentic experiences that marks poet Ziolkowski as old for his years. Words . . . come fresh as a daisy from Ziolkowski's pen . . . in shorn, unhurried sentences that bite." —*Kirkus Reviews*

"The ocean is mythical, both friend and foe, and Ziolkowski's descriptions of the duplicitous Atlantic are so gorgeous that they literally provoke goose bumps. . . . *On a Wave* is like the ocean itself—a purring pet one minute, a rough beast the next. As quiet as much of it is, it's a brisk read, a real page-turner. This, combined with a keen eye for just the right detail and the ability to re-create the thrill of riding a wave even for those of us who have never done so, marks the emergence of a major writer." —Peter Neil Nason, *The Tampa Tribune*

"[Ziolkowski's] talent and master of the language have allowed him to write this enjoyable memoir, equal parts surfer tale and bildungsroman. . . . Underneath the surfer veneer is a story about the disintegration of the author's family and growing up in a time (the mid-'70s) when all the old rules no longer seemed to apply . . . [a] touching, poetic book." —*Publishers Weekly*

"*On a Wave* will surely join the likes of Daniel Duane's *Caught Inside* and become a classic of surf literature. But non-surfers will enjoy this book too. It has a message for all who have loved and lost, only to love again." —Terry Tomalin, *St. Petersburg Times*

"This engaging memoir of Ziolkowski's coming-of-age under the sun and in the sea ultimately defines a surfer's childhood struggle between the harsh reality of land and the idyllic serenity of the water. The author's prose reflects the relaxed, bohemian way of life, perfectly capturing the surfer culture of the era. Ziolkowski's own life mirrors a storm swell . . . [and makes] for a perfect ride on a rough wave. This memoir makes one ache for the sea's ebb and flow, while his stirring account of an unconventional, oceanborne life reconfirms, for those who are landlocked, fantasies about the power and beauty of open water."   —*Library Journal*

"A long overdue testament to surfing's wonder years."
                                        —Matt Walker, *Surfing Magazine*

"Vivid imagery and emotionally charged recollections bring the experiences to life even for landlubbers and make Ziolkowski's religious fervor for surfing contagious. . . . This surfing memoir will find a receptive and empathic audience in anyone who has ever felt the desire to escape the doldrums of adult life and relive the glory days of freedom and youth."   —Gavin Quinn, *Booklist*

"I'm not a surfer, but I love this book. It's beautifully written, each sentence a poetic marvel. I take *On a Wave* to be not only the story of a boy's obsession with surfing, but the story of his search for aesthetic experience; the book presents—in the form of an accessible, graceful, hypnotic narrative—a philosophy of escapism, of our need to flee banal circumstance and seek out the trance of a high style."
                                              —Wayne Koestenbaum

"The evocation of Florida is magical in the best sense of the word, precisely mirroring the magical feeling of a child discovering his world. I was swept right along, up until the final wipeout."
                                —Tom Rayfiel, author of *Colony Girl*

"Ziolkowski masters the Zen of walking on water in a clean, lean style. His story moves gracefully yet swiftly, like sets of waves, some glassy, some choppy, alternately nurturing and brutalizing. Like the surf itself, the story left me calm yet dizzy, spent and wanting more. . . . *On a Wave* [has] humility and grace, like the soulful water gods I grew up with."   —Dr. Donna Gaines, *Voice Literary Supplement*

"Poet and essayist Thad Ziolkowski applies his chops here to a memoir of his years as a typical teenager and avid surfer, living with a distant stepfather and a doting mother in 1970s Florida. The elegant language and simple story roll with rhythm, conveying the Zen appeal of surfing and washing up gems."
                          —*Baltimore City Paper*, #10, the Year in Books

"This story of a sensitive boy's saltwater education is laconic and assured. . . . The surfing competence that Ziolkowski achieved was considerable, but this memoir is more than an account of a sport mastered. It's a sharp, self-conscious portrait of the artist as a young grommet."   —*The New Yorker*

"[Ziolkowski's] writing is vivid but understated, the pacing as natural as a set of chest-high waves. . . . This quietly mesmerizing wavelogue belongs atop the tiny—but, one hopes, growing—canon of insightful surf writing."   —Jeff Ostrowski, *Bakersfield Californian*

"Candidly observed . . . Ziolkowski's ocean is dangerous, but nurturing. His shore life is even more complex, and his account of a surfing adolescence is revealing and poignant."
                          —Annette Clifford, *Florida Today*

On a Wave

On a Wave

Thad Ziolkowski

Grove Press
New York

Author's Note: Except for those of my immediate family and certain well-known figures, the names of the people who appear in this book have been changed.

Published simultaneously in Canada
Printed in the United States of America

FIRST GROVE PRESS EDITION

Library of Congress Cataloging-in-Publication Data
Ziolkowski, Thad, 1960-
    On a wave / by Thad Ziolkowski.
        p. cm.
    ISBN 0-8021-4001-7 (pbk.)
    1. Ziolkowski, Thad, 1960—Childhood and youth.   2. Poets, American—20th century—Biography.   3. English teachers—United States—Biography.   4. Children of divorced parents—Florida.   5. Florida—Social life and customs.   6. Surfing—Florida.
I. Title.
PS3576.I564 O6 2002
811.'54—dc21
[B]   2001056498

Design by Laura Hammond Hough

Grove Press
841 Broadway
New York, NY 10003

03 04 05 06 07   10 9 8 7 6 5 4 3 2 1

To Juliana

Prologue

It was the end of my first week temping in Manhattan and I was still blinking my eyes in the fluorescent light, a bit dazed to be here. Two months earlier I'd been teaching American literature at a famous, leafy college upstate, hoping for the renewal of a one-year contract—in vain, as it turned out. Now, down to the last of my money, I was proofreading an engineering trade journal.

I squinted at the words on my computer screen, part of an article comparing different grades of cement for bridge pylons: "Machine extruded hollow core slabs . . ." Does "machine extruded" need a hyphen?

I decided to take a trip to the bathroom to think it over. I took a lot of these trips. It meant borrowing someone's security pass.

"Hey, Nance?"

She looked at me blankly. She was about my age, in her mid-thirties.

"You know what?" she was saying into the phone. "I just don't care—I don't!" She never stopped talking. I knew all about her life.

"Your pass?" I mouthed.

She waved at it as if drying nail polish.

There was a travel brochure pushpinned into the wall of her cubicle. On its map of the Caribbean, she'd drawn an arrow to Jamaica and written, "*Me* in the *SUN*—February!"

Prologue

It was August.

I buzzed myself through the security door. Coming down the hall was a man in a suit. The people who worked here were pale even by New York standards. But then there was no need to go outside: the building housed a gym, dry cleaner's, drugstore, salon. There was a mall in the basement, a walkway to the subway.

And in February, there was Jamaica.

I'd grown up in a place nearly as sunstruck—Melbourne Beach, on the east coast of Florida. That was another world altogether, though one I'd been thinking about again for the past few days, since a new magazine had commissioned me to write an essay about surfing.

Not a tenure-track subject, surfing, or something I'd considered writing about until now—now that there seemed to be nothing to lose. Yet I'd surfed for so long and with such fervor that I probably knew more about it than anything else, PhD or no PhD. I also knew that for most people it meant Jeff Spicoli and Keanu Reeves—Bro! Dude! Gnarly! That it was a bit of a joke.

The essay would run in an issue devoted to sports, but to me surfing had always been closer to religion. There'd even been a sort of pope, Duke Kahanamoku, remote and sanctified in Hawaii, the Rome of surfing. Which was probably the real reason I'd never written about it: I might fail to do them justice, those years in the pagan cathedral of ocean and sky.

I stared at myself in the bathroom mirror. "Righteous!" we used to say, and that's how we'd stood: straight, shoulders thrown back. I had an armchair slouch now. My hair, once bright, was a lank dishwater blond; teeth yellow from Camel Lights; pad of fat around my waist, care of Guinness.

But it was the eyes that troubled me most. "Stoke" is the term for a sweet sort of zeal. On the eve of a trip, a surfer might say, "God, I'm stoked about going to Fiji!"

If there was any in my eyes now, its fires were banked.

The last time I'd surfed was seven years earlier, on a lark during a vacation in Mexico. I'd still been able to do it. But first, I'd had to rent a board. In my day, not having one's own board had meant one thing: you were a tourist, an untouchable.

Nothing had changed. When I'd asked a surfer where to rent, he'd continued staring ruminatively at the waves, gestured vaguely and drawled, "There."

I'd looked back along the long coast of palms. "Where?"

He'd simply repeated the indifferent wave of his arm. "There."

Another thing I recalled: a wave that passed by out of reach the next day, hurling itself up and out in a kind of living crystalline architecture.

"It's so—*beautiful*!" I'd blurted to another surfer.

"Whoo!" he'd corrected me.

Back in my cubicle, I looked through a file of material I'd been gathering. Here was an article about surfing in the New York City area. There were surf shops in Long Island and New Jersey, even in Far Rockaway Beach, Queens, at the end of the line on the A train. New York was right on the coast, after all, though it had always seemed surfing's opposite: a grid of smoky streets, museums, bars and clubs, rivers of people.

I leafed through a recent issue of *Surfer* magazine, the Bible when I'd had religion but which I hadn't read for at least fifteen years. Waves *were* beautiful, of course. As for how people rode them now, it was more or less the same. Oh yes, I knew this world. I could feel in the pit of my stomach the speed and

G-force of the guy streaking high along a feathering blue wall. In another picture, leaning into a turn, he dragged his hand on the water and I sensed the grain of it on my own fingers, felt the board skittering across the slightly ruffled surface.

By the last page, my lips were parted, my breathing shallow. I had to suppress an urge to get up and pace around the office to blow off the steam.

What was going on here? I thought I was supposed to be over all this.

I glanced again at the article listing the Far Rockaway surf shop. There was a phone number.

I drummed my fingers on the desk, typed a hyphen into "machine extruded," deleted it, looked again at the number.

Then I picked up the phone and dialed.

"Surf shop," a woman answered.

It was like speaking into a time-travel telephone.

"Hello?" she said.

Glancing around for my supervisor, I whispered, "Um, so— how're the waves?"

"About two foot, sometimes three. Definitely ridable."

"And you're at the end of the A line?"

"You have to transfer to the S at Ozone Park."

"And you carry boards?"

"That's right." She was getting impatient.

"What about renting? Do you rent boards?"

"We don't usually, but you can talk to the owner about it. He'll be in later."

"Thanks!" I told her, "thank you!"

She'd already hung up.

I wrote the word "research" on a piece of paper, underlined it. Was I about to do what I thought I was about to do? It seemed a little crazy, but suddenly what seemed crazier was that I hadn't done it sooner.

I called my girlfriend, Juliana, at her job.

"I'm going surfing!" I whispered.

"What? Where?"

"In Queens!"

"Queens?"

"I called this surf shop in Far Rockaway, on the A—the woman there said there's surf today and—"

"Thad's going surfing in Queens!" she told someone.

"So I'm going to rent a board and, you know, go out!"

"You should!"

"You think?"

"Absolutely!"

"I'm gonna!"

"You sound excited!"

"I am!"

"Well, have fun!"

The way she said it reminded me of how little fun I'd been lately.

I hung up.

"Todd?"

My supervisor was peering over my shoulder.

"It's Thad."

"Anyway, Tad, if you're done with the proofing, we can't, you know, really be billed for whatever else you're, uh, working on, okay?"

"Well, I'm done," I told her. I doubted any bridges would collapse for lack of a hyphen.

"Great. We'll see you Monday, then."

Ten minutes later I was on the subway platform.

I studied a map. On the way to Far Rockaway ("Far Rock," I'd heard kids call it), the A train passed through three of the city's roughest neighborhoods: Bedford-Stuyvesant, Brownsville and East New York. A vision of getting off a few stops too soon— "White boy says he's looking for a surf shop!"—flickered in my head.

But when the train pulled in it was packed with working people, not thugs. This was basically the poor version of the commuter train to the suburbs: security guards, cleaning women and maintenance men on their way home from the first shift. Eyes closed in exhaustion, they rocked from side to side. More people squeezed on at Wall Street.

The train seemed to inch along, stopping frequently, and the longer it took to get there, the more unlikely it seemed that there could possibly be anything so lighthearted as surfing to be had at the end of the line. The expression "You can't get there from here" came to mind. Then we rode up into daylight at Ozone Park. I pressed my face to the window.

In the distance, a blue coastal sky flared upward. I got off on the open-air platform to transfer. I paced. I clapped my hands once then grinned at a man with a fishing pole who frowned warningly and looked through his tackle box.

Fifteen minutes later, I found myself on Far Rockaway's main drag. It was a weird place—half ghetto, half beach town from the fifties. Low cinnamon-colored public housing loomed above the side streets. To the right, traffic flashed past a sooty Wendy's and what looked like an Off-Track Betting branch, but in the direction of the ocean were festive custard and ice-cream parlors and hot-dog stands, though concertina wire was coiled along the roofs to discourage cat burglars.

For the first time in years, I broke into a jog, passing four kids with a boom box who didn't break rank until I nearly ran one of them over.

"Fuck you up!" he called, but so halfheartedly that he might have been saying "Have a nice weekend!"

Near the boardwalk was what looked like a welfare hotel, and a pair of grizzled winos or crack addicts sunning themselves like lizards on the stoop; across the street was the surf shop, a bunker-like affair with posters covering the windows. But I had to see the ocean first. I wasn't completely convinced it would be there, at least not in surfable form. I pictured an R. Crumb cartoon: dead sea, stink lines of pollution rising off it, the occasional toxic bubble bursting nastily at the surface.

But there it was, green and immense, technically the same one I'd grown up alongside in Florida. The surf was two feet, maybe three, and choppy, with whitecaps flashing along the horizon.

But there were waves, there were waves, there were waves!

I lit a cigarette, tossed it away and jogged back to the surf shop.

It was the gloomiest one I'd ever been in, but it smelled like all the others—a perfume of neoprene, resin and surf wax that made my heart flutter. There were racks of clothes and wet suits and what looked like a hundred boards to choose from in a showroom in back.

Behind the counter was a woman engrossed in an issue of *Cosmopolitan*.

"Hi!" I said, out of breath.

"Hi." She glanced up then went back to reading.

"I'm the one who called about an hour ago—"

She frowned.

"Anyway, I really want to rent a board, if possible—"

"Well, like I said, we don't usually rent."

"You said I could try talking the owner into it," I reminded her.

"Oh. He'll be back in a minute."

"Great! Would you tell him I'm back here looking at boards?"

"You got it."

I went into the showroom and stalked down the aisles of boards, running my hands over their rails, hefting them. They had grown sexier, sleek and potato-chip thin, and most were shorter than in my day, with hard rockers and three fins instead of one. They were also three times the cost, ranging upward of six hundred dollars.

Round-nosed long boards, like the tanker I'd learned on in 1970, hung from the ceiling and stood in racks, there having apparently been a renaissance of this style. I hefted one. They were far lighter than the originals. Mine had nearly bashed in my skull a few times.

The owner walked over. "Interested in a long board?"

He was in his late forties, balding, chubby.

"I'm more of a short-board man," I huffed. I couldn't seem to catch my breath.

"I hear you," he said, as if humoring me, "but a long board's your best bet for the surf around here."

"Well, see," I told him, "I was hoping to *rent* a short one, though—I know you don't usually—but I grew up surfing and I'd bring it back in one piece, so—"

"Yeah," he said. "I don't do that." The tone was: what sort of idiot do I look like?

"Even if I leave my wallet and stuff as collateral?"

"Look," he said, flipping a hand in the direction of the street, "this is Far Rockaway."

I spread my arms. "But I'm not from Far Rockaway!"

"Check these out." He led me to a rack along the back wall. "They're on sale."

I read the decals on their decks: Fat Albert . . . Surfboards Australia . . . Plastic Fantastic? I'd owned a purple Plastic Fantastic when I was thirteen. How unexpected it was to see the druggy cartoon-creature logo again. But hadn't these lines stopped coming out in the seventies?

"When did they start making these again?"

"Nah." He snickered. "They didn't—I just got the rights to use the logos. It's a nostalgia thing."

"Ah," I said, "aging baby boomers and all that?"

He winked.

"So who shaped them?"

"Oh, my people," he said vaguely.

I looked the boards over again. This decal scheme was cheesy, like putting Karmann Ghia hood ornaments on a generic car from the nineties. On the other hand, I'd never been much of a purist.

Worried suddenly that it was getting late, I asked the owner for the time. He consulted a waterproof wristwatch: "Four forty-five."

I may have avoided thinking much about surfing since I quit, but I sure dreamed about it a lot. They treaded the border of nightmare, these dreams, with most of the action being composed of anxious attempts to go surfing, usually as the light failed. I'd had one the other night: I was trying to find a board so I could go out before the sun went down. I finally did, but the waves were coming in through the lanes of a bowling alley, and just as I was figuring out how to catch them, the board turned into a pool cue.

The events of the afternoon—the hive-like office, the endless subway ride, now this strange shop in Far Rockaway—resembled nothing so much as one of those dreams.

More or less at random, I chose the faux Surfboards Australia. It cost $280. With a pair of baggies, a leash and board bag, the price would be well over three hundred.

From an ATM machine up the street, I withdrew the limit, $400. I felt giddy.

"Esteemed former colleagues of academe," I thought. "I am now about to blow my last college paycheck on a surfboard."

They replied in the mournful tones of a Greek chorus: "This hardly comes as a surprise to us."

When I got back to the shop, a boy of about eleven, scrawny and freckled and sunburned, stood at the counter with his father, who had wallet in hand and a look of tight-lipped reluctance on his face. If there'd been a thought bubble over his head it would have said, "How was I to know the kid would mow all those lawns?"

With a sigh, the father strode into the back room.

The boy turned to follow, but then, as if he couldn't contain himself a second longer, he beamed at the clerk and fairly bellowed, "I'm gonna get a *surfboard*!"

I nearly broke up laughing. This was stoke at its purest, a white-hot flame. I wanted to catch his eye and smile encouragement, but he was already moving away.

I grabbed a pair of baggies from the rack and changed into them in a booth, stuffing my pants and underwear into my book bag as the owner bore my board and leash out to the counter.

"So where'd you learn to surf?" he asked when I emerged from the changing room.

"Down near Cape Canaveral—you know Melbourne Beach?"

"Sure, yeah, I get down there every once in a while in the winter."

"Yep," I said as I tied the leash to the tail of the board, "I was hard-core back then. I used to surf contests and everything."

Now why was I telling him this? True, he might give me a better deal on all this equipment if he knew I'd once been "serious." But that wasn't it.

I'd once surfed on a team, riding "for" a manufacturer from whose shop I could pick any board I liked, free of charge. Now I was nobody. There was no reason I should be treated any differently. Yet my ego, like an unhappy ghost, cast about for its former place.

Cringing inwardly, I heard myself allude to my days as a team rider.

"Is that right?" said the owner.

Then he punched at a calculator. "Board, baggies, leash, board bag, plus tax. Rounded down," a glance at me to be sure I appreciated this munificence, "that comes to $375."

I counted out the money.

"Oh, I'd better buy some wax," I said a little glumly, holding out a bill.

He waved it away. "I'll throw in a couple of bars."

It was the same brand I'd used in the seventies: Sex Wax, shaped like a hockey puck.

"Have fun," said the owner as I headed for the door.

Fun. Had it ever, even in the beginning, been that simple?

Outside, I looked at the sky and let the question drop. There was enough light for two or three hours of surfing, and here, like a rolled-up flying carpet, I had my own board again. It was as if a spell had been lifted.

I hustled down the empty sidewalk. The wind had died and the waves were glassier and a little better than before. Oh boy, oh boy.

Then my shoe crunched on a crack vial and I decided it might be better to move down the beach a bit.

I ran along the bike path for a block and a half, kicked off my shoes and socks, fell to my knees on the beach, tore the plastic wrapping from one of the bars of Sex Wax and began rubbing it on the deck.

Down by the water, a man digging in the sand with a boy and a girl looked over at me curiously then smiled. I smiled back. But I was already smiling.

A roar poured from the sky. I looked up to see a jumbo jet lumbering in from the ocean. It was trailing black exhaust and flying so low I could nearly read the name of the airline on the fuselage. It scraped past a cluster of public housing units and entered the mauve haze above Queens.

I scanned the surf. There was a middle break about thirty yards out but I decided on the shore break, where the waves were shifty and short but had more punch. I would also be able to keep a better eye on my stuff.

I wrapped the leash around my ankle, peeled off my shirt and ran down the sand. The man and two kids stopped digging to watch me plunge into the shallows like a horse.

The warm foamy water spattered my thighs and baggies. I held the board out in front of me and leapt, floating briefly, and when I came down and started paddling, a deep *Ahhhh!* rose from me like a vapor, all the toxins of New York, the cigarette smoke and second-guessing, alcohol and elbow-throwing and worry about work. Every cell in my body opened its mouth in astonishment and sang with happiness.

This truly was the same Atlantic I'd grown up in. The rhythm of the water, the way the waves moved through the bluish late afternoon light—it was like opening a book to a poem I'd memorized in childhood.

After a minute, a wedge-shaped peak lurched up in front of me. I turned and paddled for shore. I noticed the pressure of my chest on the board, the spray in my face, a blade of light on the glassy surface below.

Then, as it gathered me up, I hopped to my feet. It was going to be a short ride. Sucking everything up into itself, the wave prepared to close out in shallow, sand-choked water.

My mind went blank; I leaned into a turn and rose back up the face of the wave. Then, without really deciding to, I attempted an off-the-lip—which was a bit like climbing on a bike for the first time in forever and trying to pop a wheelie.

But I did it. Or rather, it did itself: the nose of the board punched through the crest of the wave and snapped back around and at the bottom I stayed on my feet, bouncing up and down in the knee-high white water before flopping off the board.

When I surfaced, another jet was bearing down on Queens. I'd forgotten where I was.

I looked back at the beach—at the housing projects, the man and kids. It was all still there, of course, but I was seeing it as through a membrane. Land no longer seemed real.

The ocean did, though. Even here at the foot of a crumbling Babylon, it was alive and well.

Paddling back out, I heard again the boy in the shop announcing that he was going to get a *surfboard*. As if he'd just learned that his soul was *immortal*.

I was hearing other voices, too, waves calling—*over here! No, over here!* I heard my own voice as a boy, high-pitched and ecstatic—*Whoo! All right, now!*—and those of my friends, when I first discovered surfing, and that it could save me.

One

I remember the light. In Florida, sunlight is a force. What I mean is something else as well, though—the light of my being nine-going-on-ten, in Indian Harbour Beach, in 1970; the light of my parents' recent divorce and the presence of a strange man; the light of NASA glinting on the chrome of cars along A1A; the light of long straight hair on both men and women, of speed and acid; the light of music like "Won't You Marry Me, Bill"; the light of Tang, Pam and Pop-Tarts; the light of Vietnam.

By temperament, I was a conservative child, and not particularly well suited to the times. Dreamy, aloof, a bit priggish, I inclined to bursts of enthusiasm and monomania. In Washington, D.C., where my father was a classics professor, the shearing, operatic quality of the politics, the assassinations and race riots and war protests, some of which I witnessed peering from the window of our apartment as the city burned, troubled rather than exhilarated me. But then my parents' marriage was also quietly coming apart as the sixties peaked, and the cracking of this foundation surely made it hard to relish other, desirable collapses.

But if I held back watchfully, my younger brother, Adam, shimmied to the conga drummers in Dupont Circle wearing nothing but a loincloth, struck up conversations with homeless men and lived most of the time in a Tarzan fantasy. He was the darling of the hippies, of course, a true flower child, but he mortified me.

We spent the summer and fall that year, before coming to Indian Harbour Beach, with our mother's parents in Selma, Alabama. She was wrapping things up in D.C., probably, solidifying her new relationship with our stepfather-to-be. I didn't mind. I loved the South, the woods and rivers and farms.

My father also grew up in Alabama, in Montevallo, where his father had been a professor of music at the college. Walking in the forest there, we were always pausing to roll back logs in the hopes of finding the exquisite ring-neck snake. Now I wanted to be a herpetologist like Ross Allen, and read his and other books on reptiles with nerdy avidity. I liked the names (moccasin, copperhead, reticulated python), the beauty of the patterns, the danger. People usually found my interest in snakes creepy and ill-advised, and I liked that too.

That summer in Alabama, I caught a milk snake—it was like finding a jewel on the ground—and tadpoles that escaped as frogs, and a newly hatched snapping turtle, perfect as a locket carved of dark wood. But in autumn the woods turned drab, melancholy—as if, with the falling of the leaves, the outline of my father's absence grew unmistakably clear.

So I watched TV, *Dark Shadows* and game shows, especially those played out on brilliant beaches in California or the Bahamas. Before the divorce, we had always gone to the shore in summer; catching the first whiff of salt on the breeze blowing through the open windows, I would stick my head out like a dog, bounce in my seat, shout. It hurt to be so close yet not quite there, hurt personally, as if the earth were teasing me with its vast distances. And when the car finally stopped, I would leap out and, shadowed by Adam, sprint into the water as if on fire.

Watching the TV beaches in the gloom of late afternoons, I thought, "I'm going to a place like that, and not just for a vacation—*forever*." For if the divorce was a sort of death, and Alabama purgatory, then Florida was surely paradise.

————

And here we finally are, on its fabled sands, where we'll live forever. It's the first morning, as if it will always be morning. Yet rather than running into the arms of the water, I'm holding back watchfully. Nothing is quite as I imagined it would be, neither the "we" nor the beach.

In my father's place, there is Pat, his opposite: dark where my father is fair, analytical where he is contemplative, short-tempered where my father is gentle to a fault. My father is tall, with a flat chest and broad, sloping shoulders; his totem is a book so old it leaves behind a particulate residue of leather and crumbled paper. Pat is also tall but barrel-chested, with narrow shoulders and powerful legs and rump; his totem is a gold Cross pen.

He has unhooked the leash from the collar of our big black standard poodle, Paris, and is backing away, one hand aloft. He's wearing dark prescription sunglasses, a white windbreaker, jeans, deck shoes. Yet another way in which he is my father's opposite: the clothes match and remain neat. His nose is also neat, pinched. The corners of his mouth are cast down. He grew up in Wichita, Kansas.

"Pa-ris," he says warningly. "Stay!"

Adam joins in. "*Stay,* Paris!"

My brother's hair is straight and cut in a bowl shape; when he's frowning like this, he brings to mind a blond Moe of the Three Stooges. He's seven.

The dog peers at them with a torn, feverish expression. He's a little daft. Mom adopted him from the Humane Society in D.C. He's begun to whine and raise himself up.

Adam moves closer. "You *stay*, Paris!"

He loathes Pat but is often underfoot, as now, as if perversely drawn to him.

"Adam, dammit," Pat says, "you're confusing him!"

"Adam," Mom says, "why don't you come over here, by me?"

He ignores her.

Pat says, "Sit, Paris!"

And Paris lowers his haunches back to earth.

"Good boy!" they say in unison.

Then a seagull drifts seaward overhead and like a sprinter out of the blocks, the dog is off.

I stifle a giggle.

"Paris!" Pat snarls. "*Come* here!" He lashes his thigh with the leash and stalks off down the beach.

"Paris!" Adams echoes, running ahead. "*Come* back!"

With the air of bystanders, Mom and I turn away.

She's wearing sunglasses and a floppy white hat. She has a swan-like neck, kind blue eyes, a lovely smile, blond hair that falls to her shoulders. If she had a totem it would be the book on her bedside table, a book about psychology or astrology or psychic phenomena. But she's my mother and so beyond totems.

We walk down near the water and sit on a berm of sand carved out by uprushing foam.

"Is it always like this?" I ask her.

"Like what?"

"Cold!" I squeeze my upper arms like a bad actor. The sun is weak, small and flat as a coin in the hazy sky. I expected to be slathering on Coppertone in the shade of a thatched hut.

"I told you it gets cold this time of year."

She did, I just assumed she was mistaken. How could Florida be cold? She also said she saw surfers here when she visited. So where are they?

"Too cold for surfers?"

She purses her lips at the insinuating tone. "They're probably all in school."

"But if it weren't a school day, would they surf these waves?" It's like a bridge is being detonated in sections when they break. Lines of pelicans, flapping their wings, arch upward like spines to avoid being doused.

"It looks too rough."

"Oh, I don't know," I bluff, thrusting out my lower lip and tilting my head to one side. "Maybe I'll give it a try later."

"You most certainly will not."

"We'll see about that," I mutter.

"I beg your pardon?"

"Nothing."

The beach is hung with curtains of salt spray and there are other people out for strolls, but I can distinguish Pat by his quick steps, the way his arms swing like a samurai's or weight lifter's. That's Adam circling him like a horsefly.

"Should I help?" I'm trying to redeem myself.

She looks down the beach. "No one can catch that dog. He'll come back when he's tired out."

That's what I thought she'd say, but the offer has softened her. It never takes much.

Are we close? Not exactly. I'm usually too busy testing my strength for much beyond the occasional backward glance in search of her applause. All I have ever had to do for such approbation is, in effect, to be—grow, play, be curious. I'm Columbus to her Queen Isabella: my devotion and loyalty are enormous but remote.

I glance at her surreptitiously now, remembering something. To get here from Alabama, we drove, stopping on the way in Panama City, where we used to go in the summer with my father. I was floating offshore with Adam on a blow-up raft when I caught sight of Mom and Pat in a passionate embrace, upper bodies lifted off the towel and crushed hungrily together, *From Here to Eternity*.

I'd never seen her like that with my father. And I find myself wondering a terrible thing: has some sort of *Dark Shadows* transformation come over her? Who is this Pat character?

In his favor, of course, is the fact that he got the job in Florida. But deep down I believe this to be my mother's doing, the result of a deal she cut with God or Destiny because it's what I've always wanted, to live in Florida, and moving here is too clearly a kind of payment or compensation for the divorce and for Pat himself. Though I'm also hoping Florida will cancel him out, the way the salt spray is steadily making it harder to see him.

A swath of foam deposits a stick of driftwood and some kind of jellyfish, like chopstick and sea dumpling.

What else can I do? I pick up the stick and poke at the tangle of bright blue tentacles, the clear slimy pouch.

I look at Mom. "What's this?"

"It's a Portuguese man-of-war and they're poisonous, so stop."

I prod it. "Why?"

"Because it might pop and spray you. It's poisonous."

I heave a sigh and toss the stick into another tongue of foam. A gull's shadow ripples across the beach and a crab the color of the sand darts into a hole, then another. They're everywhere, I see now, crabs and holes.

"Do you think snakes use these holes?"

"What holes?"

Dad would know this. I wonder where he is now, what he's doing, though I can't mention him. It's there in the air, a tacit prohibition.

I'm about to dash after a crab when I notice someone out of the corner of my eye.

"Mom, a surfer!"

I walk over to him. He's wearing blue jeans and a jean jacket. There's a wet suit slung over the board.

"Are you going in?"

He glances at me, back at the water. "I was thinking about it." The frayed tips of his hair blow across his mouth.

A wave rises, light cast across its face in a single bar.

"But it's closing out."

"Yeah," I say.

He shifts his wet suit on the board, and I see that in the middle of the board is a drawing of a naked woman, her long hair wrapping across her breasts then around the front again across her hips then once more across the ankles and below her feet. In a box is written "The Rapier."

Or is it "The Raper"?

But he's shifted his wet suit again. I search his face for a sign. He does have a beard stubble, a vaguely criminal air.

Then he turns and goes back up the beach. I watch him disappear through a gap in the palmettos. What does a surfer do when he's not surfing?

I return to Mom. "That surfer?"

"See, he knew better than to go out in this."

"It's closing out."

"What?"

"That's what he said."

"There's probably a riptide."

"He said he would give me lessons, though."

She glances after the surfer.

"But he said I had to get my own board first."

"I see. Where are you going to get the money for a surfboard?"

As I'm trying to think of a reply, a wave breaks close to shore. The foam is going to wash up over our ledge of sand, but I say nothing.

Mom hops to her feet. "Damn!"

Tongue lolling, Paris trots up and stops to shake himself, followed by Adam, who lifts the dog's front paws and stands it up. It's taller than he is.

"I love you, Paris!" he shouts.

Here comes Pat. He's wrapped the leash around his wrist to whip the dog.

"Mom?"

She's checking to see whether anything in her purse got wet. I want to ask about getting a board before Pat arrives.

"Mom?"

She looks up and reads my mind.

"We'll see."

———————

Pat says, "Hey—enough TV for now." It's the next day. "How about a little help? Take out this trash."

I shuffle into the kitchen.

"If it's not too much trouble."

I don't reply. My sole weapon is acting, as he calls it, "put-upon"—sullen silences, sighs, slumped shoulders.

I carry the plastic bag of trash out through the sliding-glass doors, cross the patio and open the heavy wooden gate to the stall. Flies swirl into the air and lime-green lizards, anoles, scatter across the gray boards.

Slack-jawed, I let the bag drop. In pet shops this species costs seventy-five cents. You see them clutching plastic branches under heat lamps, grayish, eyes closed, spirits broken.

Like coins falling through my fingers, they're darting out of sight. Not that I want to sell them—just catch a few. Which is true, but I think the thought at high volume. Animals, I'm convinced, are able to listen in on my mind, and know my heart by the tone of my actions.

As I lift the lid of a trash can, another flings itself over the lip and vanishes under the fence. As a sign to its brethren, I make no move to catch it. With snakes, this nonchalance has to approach indifference. That's what Dad always said when we failed to see any on our walks in the woods.

But things will be different in Florida. If the trash stalls are leaping with lizards, imagine the swamps and woods and fields! I drift into my fantasy of being a world-famous boy herpetologist, with my own amphitheater snake pit on the edge of the Everglades, the seats filled with children and their parents, see myself casually taunting water moccasins with the toe of my sneaker.

Poor Dad. Left behind in the city, he'll miss this great and inevitable rise to glory. Part of me wishes he could be here to hunt alongside me through the mangrove swamps and grasslands. We could divide the reptilian bounty between us, father and son bestriding Florida and the world of herpetology.

But another part of me feels, cloudily, the opposite: that he should be excluded from the wealth of this new world and learn about it only in bits and pieces, enviously and from afar.

A flash of green breaks the trance. I pin it against a plank but the tail snaps off, lashing back and forth with a sickening life of its own, and the lizard itself escapes.

Tossing the tail away, I notice a scaly claw on the top board of the stall; backing up, I see a large male sunning there, its sagging raspberry throat beating. He regards me with the scornful lizard look I find so endearing.

I feint toward the door of the stall as if to leave, then lunge upward. He leaps, hits the concrete with a smack and scuttles under the fence.

I clap my hands in delight, go upstairs to my room and change into a pair of thick socks to go snake hunting in.

Mom and Pat are unpacking boxes in the kitchen. I take a garbage bag from the closet.

Mom says, "What's that for, honey?"

Pat pauses to hear what I'll say; it nearly makes me forget or want to change my mind.

"Snakes and stuff."

"Have fun," she says.

Every "town house" is the same: brick, two stories, wooden shutters painted white, rust stains on the sidewalk where the front ends of cars drip sea spray and rainwater.

There are no trees in the vacant lots near A1A, just weeds and palmettos, and I have to search to find a stick to poke around with. I walk stealthily, trying to ignore the traffic noises drifting over from the highway. The bushes rustle—a mockingbird. I tap a rusty can—a blue-tailed skink jets out. I'm expecting to come upon a pygmy rattlesnake, even an alligator.

After a while I stop, wipe the sweat from my eyes with the hem of my sweatshirt and look around. The fields are silent in the pale winter sunlight. A carpet of sandspurs has collected on my socks, canvas sneakers, pants cuffs. Picking them off, my fingers get pricked and bleed.

I walk inland. Here it's all houses and yards. There are a few promising drainage ditches, though. People driving past peer at me suspiciously as I pick my way down their steep weedy banks. Other than some minnows, the only thing moving is a rat, which I chase into a long pipe, running in a crouch through a rill of water.

When I come out the other side, I'm lost. The houses all look alike, the winding streets ending in cul-de-sacs. I'm on the verge of panic when I come to an intersection, see a pet shop on one corner and go inside.

The owner tells me how to get home; calm now, I browse among the cages and tanks. There's a chameleon for sale. It has horns and prehensile claws, and its conical eyes move independently, one of them tracking a cricket on the glass of the aquarium, the other following me. I want it, of course, but it costs more than I've ever paid for a pet—thirteen dollars. I'll have to beg Mom.

On the way home I pick some yellow flowers to butter her up with. I'll present them with a flourish and do my Dean Martin imitation: "Everybody/loves somebody/sometime!"

"Mom?" I call.

Adam's lying on the carpet, engrossed in one of his tattered Tarzan books.

Flowers behind my back, I mount the stairs.

"Mom?"

The bedroom door is closed. I listen, raise my hand to knock, listen again. Silence. Perhaps a faint hiss of sheets. I tiptoe away.

I begin a note to her at the kitchen table, a poem about the chameleon and the flowers, but a wave of embarrassment comes over me and I crumple the paper and toss it in the wastebasket.

I walk to A1A, scamper across to the loose sand on the beach side, stabbing my stick into the palmettos and sea oats in the hopes of flushing something.

The surf is a cold green, smaller than yesterday but still ominous. There are patches of choppy water out to the horizon, some of which might be made by fish, or even a single massive predator whose spiny parts disturb the surface here and there for miles. Near shore, domes of coral break the surface of the foamy water like a colloquy of misshapen heads.

There's a woman stooped over down by the water's edge, and a man wearing headphones, holding some kind of flat instrument just above the sand. Otherwise the beach is empty, presumably because it's another school day.

I test the freezing water with my hand, find a skate's black leathery egg casing, sniff it, drop it into my garbage bag, then chase the impossibly quick ghost crabs into their holes until, to my astonishment, I find myself walking beside a baby sea turtle.

It's hauling itself toward the water, plunging into footprints then back up and over, like a tank in the desert. Not many of these babies survive, I've read, which is probably why there's also a law against catching them. I look up at a pair of seagulls circling overhead and wonder if they've seen it too.

But my Snake World on the edge of the Everglades would be incomplete without a Sea Turtle Wing. I imagine this baby giving birth to hundreds like itself, each of which I'll ultimately free, riding on their backs along a river to the ocean each summer, a world-renowned event to which people flock from all over, lining the banks to watch.

The woman looking for shells is farther off now; the man with the headphones has turned away.

I grab the turtle, slide it into the bag and stroll casually up the beach, all but whistling, across A1A and then back home.

"Did you catch anything?" Mom calls from the kitchen.

"Not much."

I carry my ten-gallon aquarium to the bathroom and run the bathtub faucet into it.

Pat looms in the doorway.

"What's up?"

"Fish aquarium."

He bends to run his finger along the metal of the aquarium. I smell his cologne and sweat. "That tank will rust."

"That's okay."

"Oh, 'that's okay.' Well, you're the expert."

When the tank's half full, I stagger back to my room with it in both arms, water sloshing over the edges, set it on my chest of drawers, lock the door and drop the turtle in.

It sinks like a stone and I hold my breath, worried that it might be in shock or in some way defective. This is the first time it's been in the water—which is kind of sad, isn't it, to swim your first strokes in captivity?

It paddles to the surface in an arc, breaks the surface and breathes. Its eyes are large and expressive, like a person's. Almost instantly it reaches the wall of the tank and turns to swim back toward the other wall.

Someone tries the door.

"Let me in!"

It's Adam. I open the door as he starts to ram it with his shoulder, and he stumbles in. I lock it again.

He goes straight to the tank. "Ooh!"

"You can't tell anyone."

"How come?"

"Because it's against the law to catch them."

He frowns thoughtfully.

We watch the turtle swim from one end of the tank to the other. It's getting exhausted.

I reach into the tank and pluck it out.

"Let me hold it!"

He looks into its eyes.

"It's afraid."

"It won't be once it's used to us."

I take the turtle back, but as I start to return it to the tank I feel awful and sit down on the edge of my bed. It never stops paddling the air.

I place it on the bed and it begins hauling itself across, wrinkling the green corduroy covers. It's headed, I realize, in the direction of the ocean.

That does it.

"Come on."

I put the turtle back in the bag. We creep downstairs, get out of the house without either Pat or Mom seeing us and walk back to the beach. I worry about every car we pass, but none of them is a police or a park ranger, and we make it across A1A.

The wind has died down. Two surfers wearing wet suits are kneeling by their boards, rubbing something on the surface. They look like Marvel Comics heroes.

One of them notices the bag. "Watcha got there?"

"Nothing," Adam says.

"That's not what it looks like!" the surfer calls. "Punk!"

Adam stops. "Who you callin' 'punk'?"

They break up laughing. "You, punk!"

I pull him by the arm.

"Come on back, punk!"

Down by the water, a tongue of foam licks my sneakers. I take them off, hand them to Adam, roll up my pants, then take the turtle out of the bag. Its front fins row the air.

I wade into the shore break, holding the turtle at waist level, then, stepping off a shelf of some sort, I gasp and hold it higher.

"Thad!" Adam shouts, imitating Mom, "that's far enough!"

I grope my way onto a head of coral, seawater pouring off

the hem of my sweatshirt, and just before a wave hits, I fling the turtle as hard as I can.

I wonder whether it will survive all the things I've been reading about in a paperback called *Seashores:* birds, barracuda, needlefish, blue fish, tarpon, pompano, dogfish, crabs, adult sea turtles, eels, sharks.

It hits the water with a tiny splash.

Well, it has a little head start now, which I hope balances out the evil of having captured it.

Then out of the corner of my eye I notice something big moving out in the waves. My heart jumps and I put up a hand and squint, prepared to see anything—a sea monster trailing a thousand feet of tail behind it.

It's a surfer paddling for a wave. He's wearing a black wet suit. The board is white. Splashes flare up from his hands.

He's moving forward, toward the beach, but he's also slipping backward up the face of the wave, which turns a lighter green as it grows. Just when it looks like he's going to disappear over the top of the wave, the surfer is standing.

It's like a magic trick. He was lying down, now he's standing up.

He hangs there at the very top, seeming to go neither forward nor backward, then swoops like a hawk down the wave, leaving a white trail in the shape of a smile.

———

It's my first day of school at Apollo Elementary, named in honor not of the god but, like so much else in the area, the space program. Seen from a surfboard a few years later, the match-like flame of a rocket pulsing upward into the sky from Cape Canaveral will be as banal as a rainbow, remarkable at best for how unremarkable it has become. But at this point it's all new to me and, with the lunar landing barely six months old, to the world at large as well. Peering up at the school's name, spelled out in stainless steel letters, I feel as much on the threshold of an astronaut training program as the second half of the fourth grade.

There are palm trees on the lawn. I run my hands over the coarse trunks. Adam has stayed home sick so I'm here alone.

When kids begin coasting up on their bikes, I station myself near the doors, which are still closed. Half the blacktop is in shadow, the other half in an intense orange sunlight, which is reflected in puddles of rainwater. Staring into it makes my eyes feel colorless and strange, like a pair of glass eyes in a glass of water.

"Hey, Fatso."

I turn around. There are three of them. The boy in the middle cocks his head to the side and inquires, in faux-naïf singsong, "Fatso, why are you so fat?"

I gaze down at the watery reflection of my face in his glasses and wonder what I'm supposed to say to this. To some degree he's right, though "fat" is an exaggeration. In Selma, I gorged myself on my grandmother's southern cooking—fried okra, pans of buttery rolls, hush puppies, black-eyed peas, catfish, lemon meringue pie—and now my clothes are tight and I feel ill at ease in my body.

"Huh, Fatso?" the boy insists. "Why?"

He shrugs with ugly false modesty at having "stumped" me and turns to smirk at the kid on his left.

"Hit him now," I tell myself, "while he's looking away." For part of third grade I went to a ghetto school in D.C., and this is the kind of thing I learned. When the boy I sat next to became my friend, he taught me how to play conga rhythms on the desk using the heels of my hands, then showed me his switchblade, unfolding it in his lap so the teacher couldn't see. He suggested, as a piece of friendly advice, that I get one too. I considered it. Everyone else seemed to carry some kind of weapon. I did always make sure to bring a bundle of pencils, which circulated like cigarettes in prison, a currency. There were spontaneous uprisings. I saw my teacher, a well-meaning but tentative young man, swarmed into a closet and held captive for a morning. Standing in line (and we were always standing in line), you would hear someone say, "Back up off me, punk!" and often a fight would break out. I learned to shadowbox and bluff, and to avoid looking into people's faces for more than a second.

There were four other white kids in the school, and at the end of each day we sought each other out and walked home together. One afternoon we met a black boy staggering down the sidewalk, weeping and in shock. He had been slashed with a razor and the blood stood in thick vertical red lines on both cheeks.

Not long after that, I buried my own face in a pillow on the couch and refused to go back. My parents, surprised at the extent of my misery, which I poured out all at once, enrolled me in a private school, though I got the impression that they could scarcely afford it.

Now I ball my fist but hang fire. He might be acting tough for his two friends, because I'm bigger than he is, and if I don't react they'll go away.

"Fatso," the middle boy is saying, "I asked you a question." He takes a step closer, scowling in the sunlight like a demon. I can feel the eyes of other kids on us now, hazy figures drawing nearer.

"He asked you a question, Fatso," the boy to his left says, and the middle boy reaches out with a finger and prods me in the chest. "You!"

I brush the hand away and hear myself say, "Back up off me, punk!"

In confusion, they freeze, then all three shove me at the same time. I reel backward, slip and fall on my hip in a puddle.

"Oops!"

"Sorry, Fatso!"

"Yeah, we're sorry!"

They stamp in streaks of water like chimpanzees and swagger away.

I pick myself up, avoiding the eyes of the students who have been watching the confrontation and are now shouting about it excitedly. One leg of my pants, which are brown and now make me think of shit, of having shit my pants, is soaked and gritty with mud.

As I stand there wondering whether to go home and change, the school bell rings, the doors are opened and students begin flowing into the building. I watch for a bit then numbly join them, peering into the sunny classrooms until I find mine.

The teacher, Miss Clark, is young and attractive, but as I hand her the slip of paper with my name and hers on it, which is crumpled and wet from the puddle, I see that her manner is severe. She seems to consider scolding me but then waves me to a seat.

I find a desk at the back of the room, trying to ignore my wet pants and the fact that I've been humiliated, while also feeling, obscurely, that I deserve what I got, that I'm everything those boys implied I was: fat and weak and worthless.

We read in the morning—stories about a boy who lives on the prairies in Saskatchewan, Canada, which I enjoy, and which lift my spirits—but when it's time for science, my mind wanders. I'm an indifferent student, half present at best. I still can't tell time, for instance, though that's one of the things I was supposed to have learned in private school, and my idea of using commas is to distribute them through a paragraph according to what looks right.

As Miss Clark diagrams an eyeball on the board, I borrow paper from the girl at the next desk and make drawings of sharks, of sea turtles, of Miss Clark riding sea turtles, her long hair blowing backward—

Miss Clark snatches up the pages and tears them to shreds under my nose.

"Son," she whispers, digging her nails into my forearm, "I'm going to give you a break because you're new here, but do not test me!"

Her breath smells of lipstick and coffee. I blush and stare at the nubbly flame-retardant carpet until she stalks back to the front of the class. When I emerge from my trance of embarrassment, we're studying multiplication tables, alone at first, then in pairs using flash cards.

My partner is a short boy named Joe. He has high sharp cheekbones, freckles and red bangs that fall into his eyes so that he has to toss or rake them back with his fingers. He draws, too, he confides in a whisper, and I sense that he admires me for having been made to suffer for my art. When Miss Clark leaves the room for a minute, he hastily shows me pictures from his notebook, paisley-encrusted peace signs, a seascape with surfers, leaping dolphins, all of them so assured that I feel envious despite myself and worry that my role as class artist won't be as easy to assume as it usually is.

Now Miss Clark has us arrange the desks into a circle. She wanders in the middle with a yardstick in one hand then shouts out a problem—"Four times five!"—and wheels to whack a desk with the yardstick.

"Twenty!" pipes a tiny blond boy.

"Five times five!" She spins and brings the yardstick down on my desk. I flinch and say, luckily, "Twenty-five!"

Finally we're excused for recess. Joe and I walk slowly through the hall together, like survivors, and lean weakly against a palm tree just outside the door.

After a while, he asks how my pants got wet, and as I tell him he frowns incredulously, his breath coming in puffs, as though I'm recounting a humiliation of his own that he's somehow forgotten and must now avenge.

He rakes the bangs out of his eyes and says quietly, "Show him to me."

I put up a hand against the bright sunlight, scan the seething crowds of students and finally spot the middle boy playing tetherball.

"There he is, on the blacktop."

Joe gives a toss of his bangs. "Come on!"

He stalks off on the balls of his feet, chest out, arms cocked at the elbow. Alarmed to find myself being defended, especially by someone so much smaller, I hang back for a beat as if to disassociate myself from it, then run to catch up.

When we reach the tetherball game, Joe steps into the court and catches the ball as it's going around.

"Hey!" shouts the boy.

Joe shouts, "What's your problem?"

The boy looks from Joe to me and scowls, comprehension dawning. "I don't got a problem." He sounds less than completely convinced. A knot of kids, scenting conflict, has already formed around us.

"Well, you're gonna have one if you mess with my friend!" Joe jerks his thumb in my direction then passes me the tetherball without looking, as in a bucket brigade.

The boy ponders this, cocking his head in a way I recognize queasily. "You and what army?"

Joe twists his mouth in disgust, as if at the boy's lack of originality, then springs, shoves him hard in the chest, bounces back then springs forward to shove him again, all in a blink, like a mongoose.

The boy is shaken now, and, thinking only to add a little to his misery, I launch the tetherball in his general direction. But it picks up speed along the way, rises suddenly at the end and hits him squarely on the side of the head, snapping it sideways and sending his glasses to the blacktop with a clatter.

He clutches his temples histrionically. "My glasses!"

I start toward him to help, but Joe catches my arm and leads me off solemnly, as if away from a man for whom nothing more can be done.

Cleaving through the crowd, I glance back a few times to make sure no one is pointing us out to the teachers.

Joe shrugs as if to say "Well, I guess we got away with it," then clutches the sides of his head and shouts, "'My glasses!'"

We cackle maliciously and take turns mimicking the kid's head snapping sideways. "Boom!"

"My glasses!"

The sun has dried out my pants.

A seagull swoops to snatch a potato chip from the upheld hand of a girl, then veers away shyly.

I turn to Joe. "Hey, do you surf?"

"No," he says, "but my brother, Ian, does. He's thirteen."

The bell rings and we merge with the crowd heading back in, boys with crew cuts or Beatle bangs, girls with long hair held back by barrettes.

"He has a board and everything?"

"Yeah, and a wet suit. You need a wet suit."

"I want to learn," I tell him. Then, hoping to be invited home, "Maybe he could give me some tips or something, your brother?"

My wish comes true, though not until the end of the week. In the meantime I've been to the large house of a quiet boy who has a pet gopher turtle, which he caught in one of the vacant lots. But the boy and the turtle turn out to be a bit boring, and his mother, a tall astronaut's-wife sort, seems to detect something disreputable about me, some trace of hippie city life perhaps.

Now Joe and I are walking through the neighborhood to the south of school toward his house. Here the houses are small and one-story, but each has its own lawn and driveway. Sprinklers cough three times—tch! tch! tch!—then spray in machine-gun-like arcs across the grass and into the street. We wait until the last second then dodge, and if any water grazes us, we shout, "I'm hit!"

Orange flowers, huge and papery, lie in the gutters beneath the bushes they fell from. The sky is a vast pale blue, streaked with cirrus clouds and, near the horizon, a brilliant pink jet contrail breaking up along the edges.

"You know what's gross?"

"What's gross?"

"No," Joe corrects me. "You say, 'I don't know, what?' It's a joke."

"Okay," I say. "I don't know, what?"

"Let's start over." He pauses. "You know what's gross?"

"I don't know, what?"

"When you throw your underwear against the wall—*and it sticks.*"

We laugh. "You know what's gross?"

"I don't know, what?"

"When your grandmother comes in to kiss you good night—*and she slips you the tongue.*"

When we finish laughing, Joe says, "Ian told me those. He knows tons more."

At Joe's house, his father—a fireman, he told me—is sprawled on the couch in the small living room watching television. He nods and says, "Joe. Joe's friend."

We wave and walk to the end of a hallway. Joe presses an ear against a door then knocks lightly. After a pause it's opened by Ian, who sizes us up impassively, doorman at an exclusive nightclub, then turns and crosses the room to a stereo resting on a crate.

Shirtless and barefoot in a pair of Levi's, Ian is essentially a larger, muscular version of Joe, even to the angled bangs, though the sun has bleached away all but a trace of red.

Joe nods at me and I follow him in.

"Close the door!"

The alacrity with which Joe darts back to do so leaves no doubt as to how tenuous our foothold is here.

"This is Thad," Joe announces. "He just moved here."

Flipping through the albums, Ian says, "What's happenin'?"

"Not much" is the correct reply, but I don't know this yet and am puzzled by the consternation that flickers across Joe's face when I say simply, "Hi."

As if to account for this lapse, Joe adds, "He's from Washington, D.C."

I'm turning slowly now, taking in the room. There's a small, neatly made bed and the stereo atop its crate. But it's the walls on either side that have me spellbound. Each is covered floor-to-ceiling with what looks at first like a tapestry but is actually a collage of fragments of surf posters and pages from surf magazines, a dazzle of bright whites and blues and greens, dawns, noons, twilights, arms and bodies and boards, which I see, looking back and forth between the two, first as abstractions, which they very nearly are, cascading vortices of light and dark—a kind of surfer chiaroscuro.

Next to the door behind me is the coup de grâce: a cork bulletin board bearing a mechanically precise pencil drawing of *MAD* magazine's mascot, Alfred E. Neuman, down to the typewriter lettering spelling out the motto: "What, Me Worry?"

I gaze reverently at this masterpiece until distracted by the surfboard leaning in a corner. It's without mark or color except for the words Gordon & Smith. The clear resin is like Ian's pale Irish skin, as if the board were a sibling. On the deck is a feathery layer of wax.

"What's this for?"

Ian pulls a record from its sleeve and puts it on the record player. "Traction," he says, glancing back. "It's wax."

Music, Santana, fills the room, the congas reminiscent of Dupont Circle. Looking at the jacket sleeve, Joe says, "He wants to learn to surf."

This revelation is passed over without comment. I stand staring at the board, the cold flawlessness of it, then Joe beckons to me and I sit down beside him on the carpeted floor to look at the Santana cover, a drawing of a lion's head comprised of buried images of women and breasts hidden like visual secrets, puzzles nested within other images.

There's a knock at the door, Ian calls, "Come in!" and a boy his age pokes his head into the room, says "Hey," then comes all the way in, closing the door behind him.

Joe says, "What's happenin', Petey?"

He has a long neck and raffish good looks. "Not much, punk.

"So Ian," Petey says, "did you see Cindy today?"

"Nah."

"Oh, shit," Petey says now, looking out the window above the stereo, "speak of the fuckin' devil!"

We all turn. A girl with straight blond hair and a sexy bow of a mouth is tapping on the glass with her fingernails. She waves for Ian and Petey to come outside. They both wave back with their fingers but make no move, either to open the window or go outside, and after a moment she makes a face and disappears.

"Um," I say, "I thinks she wants you to meet her outside."

"No fuckin' duh," Ian says.

Petey looks at Joe. "Where'd you find this genius?"

"Last night," Joe explains, "she puked in Ian's pup tent."

"Ah," I say, giving it what I hope is a worldly "Why didn't you say so in the first place" inflection.

To the tune of "Shave and a Haircut," Ian sings,

> *Puked in the pup tent*
> *Two times!*

and to my relief their scorn is redirected at the girl, my gaffe buried in laughter.

Joe and I turn to a neatly stacked pile of *Surfer* magazines.

"They better be back like that when you're done," Ian breaks off from his conversation with Petey to warn us.

"Okay!"

The cover of the issue on top of the pile, the most recent, dated March though it's February, shows a surfer crouched in a glittery tube, the roof of which looks like a cedar limb weighed down by fresh snow and ice. In the foreground floats a clutch of hexagonal sparkles; the water-level angle of the shot lends it a bobbing, aquatic intimacy, though the overall quality is one of stillness, an iconic hush resulting from the backlit, silhouetted form of the surfer, and the position of his hand, which is poised above the inner wall of the wave as if in benediction.

At the bottom of the picture, it says:

warning: this magazine contains sex, violence, dirty words, and sixty-foot disaster waves. may be harmful to anyone over 25.

Joe and I laugh, neither of us completely certain why, and turn the page.

———————

Mom and Pat are to be married tomorrow, Sunday, at home. She told me this a few days ago, as we drove back along A1A after shopping for school clothes in Satellite Beach, sunlight, broken up by telephone poles overhead, falling in bars across our faces.

They've been living as if they were married already, so what's the point? Have I mentioned that they have the same first name? She recently had some sort of coin pressed to memorialize it: Pat and Pat. How romantic.

For the occasion, he has driven across the state to Tampa to fetch his children, Neal and Nellie, who live there with their mother, Pat's ex-wife. Nellie is my age, Neal two years older. In Selma, Mom showed Adam and me photographs of them, slim, deeply tanned, sandy-blond kids, mouths cast down at the corners like Pat's. In the pictures they were water-skiing, looking up from paper plates piled with potato salad and barbecued hot dogs, poised midair above a blurred diving board. I glanced grumpily at the images then later, on the sly, looked again, seeing not only a version of my Floridian future but children who appeared to be enjoying the aftermath of divorce as though it were a windfall.

I find Mom reading the newspaper at the kitchen table. I pop it with my middle finger. She peers at me over the top.

"Um, Mom?"

"Um, yes?"

"Can I—?"

She raises her eyebrows. I rephrase the question. "When can I get a surfboard?"

As if she's been waiting for me to appear and put this to her, she spreads the paper out on the table. The boards are drawn in black and white and float on the page, clean and exact, like designs.

"They're a lot more expensive than I thought," she says, moving a finger from price to price, a slight, aggravating note of pity in her tone. "Look: a hundred dollars, ninety-five, a hundred and twenty, seventy-five . . ."

"I don't have to get a brand-new one," I say. "We could buy a used one to start with."

"Honey, these are the used ones."

"Oh."

I frown at the prices and the boards, as at a test question I'm unprepared for, waiting for a solution to occur to me.

When that doesn't happen, I get mad. "Well, you promised!"

"Don't yell. I said we'd see, and we will see."

"Yeah, sure!" I storm upstairs to my room, slamming the door.

It's early evening when I feel through the walls the muffled shudder of the front door closing, then hear Paris barking, Mom's voice, Pat's, the high voices of what must be Neal and Nellie.

I get up from the bed, where I've been reading my Ross Allen book, and listen at the door. Then I put a new Jackson 5 forty-five on my tiny record player and grimly turn the volume all the way up. It's bubblegum pop but sounds to my ears as cacophonous and angry as Jimi Hendrix. I mean it to reverberate against my closed door, a "keep out" sign, but also to drift downstairs as a warning of my unapproachability, my general displeasure.

But the appeal of family groups—the Jackson 5, the Cowsills, the Osmonds—is their clan unity. These are families so happy they break into song. Listening, I usually graft myself onto their lives, floating upward out of myself where I lie on the bed, corpse-like, hands folded on my chest. Today I sit in a chair and frown.

Someone is knocking. When I make no move to turn down the music or come to the door, Mom opens it.

"Thad, Neal and Nellie are here."

"What?"

She crosses the room and turns the music down. "Neal and Nellie are here." Her tone is understanding, but I don't want to be understood. I want to intimidate and disappoint.

"So?"

"Don't you want to come down and meet them?"

"I'll be down later. I'm listening to music."

"Okay, but I think you might like them."

I shrug. "I'll be down later, when I'm done here."

She goes out.

I put the needle down on the beginning of the record and turn the volume up again, but with completely different results: it sounds tinny and forced, tainted somehow. What now?

I leave it on for a few more minutes, out of principle, then go downstairs and into the living room, avoiding Pat's eyes, though I sense by his body language that he's relieved, even grateful, that I've given up my siege.

Neal and Nellie are sitting on the couch. Adam's showing them one of his Tarzan books, and when I come into the room he looks at me with a guilty start, as if he knows he shouldn't be welcoming them but can't help himself.

Mom introduces us.

"Hi," they say shyly.

"Hi," I reply glumly.

They look like their photos, only somber and uncomfortable, thanks to me.

We go out to dinner at a saloon-style pizza restaurant that serves pitchers of Coke and plays movies against one wall. Neal and Nellie and Adam and I sit at our own table. When Neal and Nellie see I'm no longer going to be difficult, they warm to me and complain about their stepfather, but he sounds merely foolish and their tone is lighthearted.

The next day, in the early afternoon, a minister of some sort marries our parents in the living room. Mom is radiant and Pat, I have to admit, looks handsome in a blue suit that gives his hair the bluish cast of dark hair in comic books.

Afterward we go swimming in the Jamestown Apartments pool. I'm the fastest, but Neal and Nellie so wow everyone poolside with flips and gainers that I end by basking in our stepsibling-hood.

That evening I find Neal curled on the couch. He has his knees pulled up to his chest and his hands tucked between his legs. I sleep like this myself but I've never seen anyone else do it and stand there watching him for a moment.

After they've gone, Mom tells me she's found an ad for an affordable used surfboard. It will be my tenth-birthday present.

"When can I get it?"

"Tomorrow, after school, when Pat gets home from work."

"What's his job?"

"He works at Tech Systems."

"Did he go to college for that?"

"He has a master's degree; do you know what that is?"

"Yes." I sort of do. Well, Dad has a PhD. "But what's he *do* there?"

"He's in the marketing department."

"Oh, so he sells stuff."

She searches my face but I keep it blank. "That's right."

It's the first time I've been alone with him in the car. He's wearing his suit and tie from work. His cheeks, in profile, are somewhat chubby and soft, but in his eyes is a tough, smoky expression. There is, as often, something on his mind, dividing his attention. It's as if he must keep one eye on the world, one eye on the thing inside. What is it? I have no idea.

The sunset above the Indian River looks like scales of dried egg yolk on a vast mauve plate.

I'm expecting a surfer of the sort I saw on the beach the first morning, but the man who answers the door looks more like Pat. He wears the same dark-rimmed glasses, short hair, sideburns, the white shirt and tie. Up closer, though, I can see that his hair has little sun-bleached wings in it. He leads us across the lawn to the garage.

"It's just been out here for the past few years," he says. He pulls up the door and jerks the string of a lightbulb. "Thar she blows."

"Wow," I say.

The board lies on the concrete floor, stretching from one end to the other. The foam is yellowish under the clear resin and fiberglass. A pair of wood stringers runs up the middle. The fin is black and worn, as if ridden in shallow water across rocks.

"It's sort of a classic at this point," the man says wistfully.

"It sure is!" I say.

"Would you be able to carry this thing?" Pat asks me.

"Sure!"

"'Sure.'" He smirks. "The expert," he says to the man.

The man smiles at me, eyebrows raised as if to say "Give it a try."

I walk to the middle of the board and straddle it. Up by the nose there's the outline of an island, and inside it, "Surfboards Hawaii."

"The kids now are riding the much shorter ones," the man says. "But this is a good beginner's board."

I wonder how he knows I'm a beginner. Mom must have told him over the phone.

I heft it. It's heavy, like solid wood. I step to one side and hoist it up to get an arm around it, the nose still on the concrete, but my fingers don't reach the rail and I can't get a sure grip.

"Well," says Pat.

"Why don't you try—" the man begins, but I'm giving the board a bump with my hip to get it farther up under my arm, and it slips.

"Whoa!"

I jump back as if to deny my connection to what's happening, and the board hits the floor with a crash that echoes off the walls of the garage, then rocks side to side, shuddering from the impact.

"Jesus Christ—easy!" Pat says, smacking his forehead with one hand.

"No, no," the man says, "that's my fault, that's my fault."

He picks up the board, glances at the tail and scoffs. "You'd have to drop this thing off the roof to ding it."

"The expert," Pat says apologetically, shooting me a glare.

I study the floor of the garage, the sparkly grit, the oil stains, one of which looks like Cuba. Or is it a diving whale?

"Here," the man says. He stoops and picks up the board and carries it out of the garage.

"Hey," he calls. He's stood the board in the grass. "Try getting it up on top of your head."

I shuffle out to the lawn.

The man turns to Pat. "I should have said you have to carry these big boards on your head."

I stand in front of the board and look up. It's at least twice my height. Curving away, the nose disappears into the sky.

I lean my forehead against it, grip the rails, take a step backward and shove. The tail swings up like a crane.

"There you go," the man says.

Pat mutters, "Jesus."

It settles onto my head. My vision reddens. I step to one side to get a better footing. My ankle wobbles.

"I'm right here, I gotcha," the man says from close beside me.

I stagger again.

Pat calls, "Watch it there!"

I find my balance. "I got it."

"There it is," the man says.

"I can carry this!"

I take another step forward.

"Easy now," says the man. "Got it?"

"I got it now," I say, willing myself to be still. I'm like a weight lifter waiting for the judge's signal.

Pat lights a cigarette. "We live three blocks from the beach," he says. "But then"—he chuckles mirthlessly—"there's the problem of getting across A1A."

The man says to me, "You look both ways before you cross, right?"

"Sure." The crown of my head is numb.

"Well?" Pat says.

Through clenched teeth I say, "Let's get it!"

"Twenty, wasn't it?" Pat says.

"It's a classic," says the man. "But for the kid here, I'll let it go for fifteen.

"From me to you," he says softly, raps twice on the top of the board and lifts it off my head.

Two

I come awake all at once, as if to a tremor, pull on Bermuda shorts and a sweatshirt and pee as quietly as I can in the bathroom down the hall. I'm hoping to slip away before anyone else wakes.

I squat beside the aquarium and rake a fingernail over the mesh lid. The chameleon remains motionless. He was the other birthday gift yesterday.

Has it died already? I tap the glass. The pebbly lid of one eye peels back like the foreskin of a penis, pivots upward at me: "You rang?"

I creep downstairs, open the sliding-glass door and look at the board. It's been here all night, while I slept, mine.

Hoisting the nose, I drag the front half of the board into the living room. Then I hear Mom's voice.

I go to the foot of the stairs. She's standing at the top, nude, face bleary and cross.

We are, or were before the divorce, a family comfortable with nudity. But she's emerging from another man's bed now, and the sight of her makes me vaguely uneasy.

"Keep it down!" she whispers. "We're still sleeping!"

"Sorry!"

There's something on her pubic hair—sperm?

"What are you doing up so early?"

"Going surfing!"

"I thought you were going to wait until we went with you."

"That surfer? He's gonna give me lessons!"

"Keep your voice down. What surfer?"

"The one I talked to that day, remember? On the beach."

"That was over a month ago." Maybe it's string.

"He said he's always there—at the beach."

She doesn't seem to believe any of this. "Well, if for some reason he's *not* there, don't you go in alone."

"Okay."

"I'm serious."

"I won't."

She studies me a moment longer. I'm ten but look twelve, thirteen. I learned to swim before I learned to walk.

It's enough. She turns and walks back down the hall. I wait until I hear the bedroom door close then I open the front door, pick up the board near the nose and drag it outside.

The gray sky is rushing inland. I need to go. One of them might open the bedroom window and forbid me. And I also simply need to go.

I don't remember getting the board up onto my head, but I find myself walking along the last row of town houses, my hands steadying the rails as in pictures of surfers from the 1960s, the *Endless Summer* poster.

A light rain rattles on the board, needles of cold water on my fingers. At A1A, a car with fishing rods sticking out the windows buzzes by in the near lane, then a station wagon with small surfboards on top passes going north, a blond head yelling something—"kook"? "gook"?—the word stretched to breaking by the speed.

My skull burns from the weight of the board. There are cars coming, but I run anyway. The board jounces, a gust of wind lifts it off my head and I cross one foot over another, scrape my toe and nearly fall.

Above the grind of downshifting, someone yells, "Come on, come on!"

I trot through the gap between the palmettos and sea oats, the ocean coming into view in jerks, whitecaps along the gray horizon, the unspeakably deep water, then the sliding gray forms of the waves, their white water sifted by the domes of coral near shore.

I walk to the edge of the water and heave the board off my head. It strikes the hard sand with a clank.

There's no one out or on the beach. To the north, a man with a fishing pole silhouetted in the mist. Foam rushes over my feet, stings the scraped toe. Do I go in alone?

A line of pelicans wheels inland. Following it I see, up by the sea oats, two surfboards planted like stakes in the sand.

I drag the board back from the water's edge and jog up the beach.

Two surfers, older than the others I've seen, are seated Indian style, smoking.

"Hi," I say.

"What's happenin'," says the one with long hair. The other has short hair, sunburned ears. They both wear plaid wool shirts and jeans.

"Are you guys going out?"

"For sure," says Long Hair. He turns to his companion. "Right?"

Short Hair seems not to have heard.

"Soon as we have another cig," Long Hair tells me.

The rain stops.

Short Hair stands up, snapping a silver lighter open and closed. "I'm gonna get a fire going." He has a southern accent.

"Definitely," says Long Hair. "Bitchin'."

"Should I get my board?" I ask.

"Get it."

I run down the beach, hoist the nose under my arm and drag it up the sand. They're crouched over a pile of trash and driftwood, blowing on a small flame.

"That's a monster you got there," Long Hair remarks and smiles at Short Hair, who's setting a Marlboro box on fire with his lighter.

"Yeah," I say doubtfully.

"Can you hang ten?"

"No way." Adding, "Not yet."

"Maybe I could try it later?"

"Sure."

He walks over and hops on the middle of my board. I feel myself blush. Is this some sort of insult?

He scampers to the nose and puts one foot over the tip. "Hang five!" Then he brings up the other foot and lets both feet dangle. "Hang—how many?"

"Ten," I say.

Back arched, he raises both arms in mock triumph. "Hang ten it is! Whoo!"

He swaggers back to the fire and chucks me on the shoulder.

"Nice board, man. I'm just kiddin' around with ya."

Rubbing his hands over the flames, he studies the surf.

"Well, shit," he says. He peels off his shirt, his jeans. He's wearing baggies underneath. "I'm going out."

He looks at Short Hair. "You comin'?"

Short Hair shakes his head. "You go ahead, buddy. I'm gonna get this roarin'."

"Righteous," Long Hair says. "Get it roarin'!"

He yanks a wet suit from under a pile of towels, shakes sand from it and struggles into it. I like the smell. It covers everything but his arms, feet and head. On the chest is a logo of a surfer on a wave and the name O'Neill.

He fastens the shoulder flap then picks up the bright pink board. It, too, looks new. Toward the nose is a cartoon figure and the words "Plastic Fantastic" in cartoon letters.

"You sure?" he says to Short Hair.

"Yeah, man. You go on."

"Righteous," Long Hair says and walks down the beach, his expression suddenly grave.

Short Hair looks up from the fire. He's rolled up his sleeves. On one forearm is a tiny tattoo.

"Doesn't know what the hell he's doin'."

I watch Long Hair place the board in the shallows. "He doesn't?"

"Never been on one of those things in his life," he says, his voice raised as if I've doubted his word. "*Says* he has, but I don't believe it."

We watch Long Hair begin to paddle. He uses both arms at once, as if rowing.

"It all comes out in the wash," Short Hair says with a smile.

A small gray peak rears up and begins to break. Long Hair paddles harder but somehow the pink board squirts free.

Long Hair fights to the surface and stands. The water comes to his waist.

"Whoo!" he shouts, pumping one arm in the air, then gallops after the board, pausing to plunge his head in the water and whipping his hair back.

"Whoo-hoo!" Short Hair replies sarcastically, raising a fist.

Long Hair grabs the board and starts back out again, twisting around after paddling a few strokes to wave us in.

"Gonna give it a go?" Short Hair asks me.

I squint at the surf in imitation of Long Hair. I nearly wet a finger in my mouth and check the wind but think better of it.

The waves look small and weak enough, but it's so choppy and cold and gloomy. I wouldn't be surprised to see the broken mast from a shipwreck sticking up out of the water near the coral.

Long Hair is floundering before a larger wave now. Maybe I really should get lessons. Maybe Short Hair would give me lessons if I ask—though if anything he looks less like a real surfer than Long Hair.

"I think I'll wait for the tide to change," I say finally.

Short Hair laughs. "The tide to change?"

"Yeah."

Suddenly his face reddens, contorts as if he's tasted something putrid.

"Boy!" It makes me flinch. "*Get* your Surfboards Hawaii ass out in that water!"

His teeth are bared, body visibly tightened. It's as if he's about to leap up and seize hold of me.

I don't know what to do. I consider running then look again at the ocean and hastily pretend to reconsider.

"Uh, what about you?"

"Me?" he says. "Who the hell asked you about me?"

"I just—"

"Don't you fuckin' worry about me!" He stabs at the fire with a stick. "Fuckin' kid, fuckin' twelve-year-old child, wondering 'what about you?' Everybody always fuckin' wonderin' about other people. When what they better do is wonder about themselves!"

He smiles at the fire, then at me. "Well, hell. As the song says, 'God bless the child that's got its own.'"

I don't know that song. I pull off my sweatshirt and walk over to my board. I want to get away from this guy.

"In other words," I hear him say as I try to get the board up onto my head.

"*In other words,*" he repeats, wanting me to look at him. I look at him.

"Can't swim," he says, scanning my face. He points at the other board by the fire. "That's his. His daddy bought 'em both, I bet."

"Oh," I say.

"I'm just here on business, you might say."

"Oh, okay," I say.

He stands, thrusts out his hand, arm flexed. "Lester."

Cautiously I walk back to the fire and take his small hand. He rolls mine into a soul shake and squeezes hard, pulling me close. He smells of cigarettes and something else—cologne or beer.

"Thad," I say.

"What's happenin', Stan?"

"Not much." The tattoo is two words in blue ink: "Semper Fi." Latin, I think, missing my father.

"Had a buddy named Stan," he says, looking past me at the surf. He still grips my hand tightly. "Stan could swim his ass off."

"Well," I say, pulling my hand free, "I'm a pretty good swimmer."

"Good," he says, chuckling, and lifts his chin toward the surf. "Maybe you can save him."

The pink board is washing in again and Long Hair himself is nowhere to be seen. Then he pops up, hoots, stumbles on something and goes under again.

I walk back to my board.

"Later, Stan," Lester says.

"Later."

"Get some for me."

"Okay."

"Ho, Stan—"

"Yeah?"

"Tell that motherfucker I'm gone."

"Okay."

"Tell him for me."

"I will," I promise.

I drag the board to the water and lift the nose over the first wave of the shore break, which smacks my chest, so cold it almost knocks the wind out of me. I smell the smoke from the fire rise from my shorts.

Then I climb on and paddle. The waves appear much bigger from the board, as if I'm entering an altogether different ocean.

I crane around to see how far out I am. The beach is right behind me!

Lester shouts something, waving me on.

I paddle. I hear my breath echoing, wind blowing across my ears, water sloshing and chattering against the board. It passes into me as vibrations.

I paddle through dashes of white water, the board rearing like a seesaw. A wave rises into the air as if ascending an invisible ladder, but sliding sideways too. The crest thins out until daylight leaks through, then it vanishes into the sky and disembowels itself.

I put my head down on the board, grip the rails and hold on tight. The white water heaves the board back toward the beach, rushing between me and the deck and into my nose and mouth, snarling at me. It drags me halfway into the water, then relents and I climb back on, coughing up foam.

Another wave comes and the same thing happens, then once more, and then there's only ocean, eerie without a wave.

It must be only five or six feet deep, but there, all the way out where the whales are, and the sharks—what about that? Is there even a bottom out that far?

Then out of nowhere a peak appears. With pounding heart I plunge my arms into the water. The board glides over the crest.

"Whoo!"

Long Hair is sitting up on his board as in a saddle. When I reach him he puts out his hand.

"Bill," he says. A swell knocks his board against mine. I check to make sure a bigger wave isn't on the way.

"Your friend? He said to tell you that he was gonna go."

Bill jerks around toward the beach and nearly flips his board. "Whoa," he tells himself.

Then he yells, "Lester!," drawing out the name. It hurts my ears. I make a face and look back at the beach. Lester is walking over the top of the bluff.

"Lester!" Bill yells again, and starts paddling in his rowboat style toward the beach, chin resting on the deck.

"I'll be right back," he tells me.

A wave is coming.

"Hey," Bill calls over his shoulder as the wave rolls underneath and lifts my board. "We can drive down south in my van!"

Beginning to break, the wave lifts Bill up and sets him down so that his legs splay and the tip of the board and his upper body dip under.

"To Sebastian Inlet!" he says when his head comes up.

I look seaward. A bigger wave is coming. A seabird flutters at the crest as if to pluck something from it.

I paddle a little farther out and consider trying to catch this wave but then let it pass. It groans and leaps and I'm relieved I didn't try to ride it.

I sit up on the board and look down at my white legs dangling into the fanlight, then out again at the horizon. Wisps of bright cloud drift across a storm bank.

It starts to rain hard, a low roar, the pelted water leaping, forming a gray cone around me. I can see neither horizon nor beach, but it's oddly comforting within it. I feel safe, invisible.

I think, "I'm alone out in the ocean."

The rain stops suddenly. The beach is empty.

Now a school of minnows is flinging itself forward, animate gold pieces, and as I paddle to avoid the fish and whatever must be pursuing them, a small wave lifts up. There's a hissing sound as it catches hold of the board, heaving it up and up then slinging it toward the beach.

I try to stand but only get up on one knee, like I'm posing for a photograph in the first row of a football team. Then the nose of the board plunges under and I somersault into the water.

The wave rolls me over and down to the bottom and I push off and pop up, smiling. That wasn't so bad!

I look around. Where's the board?

Something hits me on top of the head so hard it feels like a TV, like a safe dropped off a building in a cartoon.

I see stars and slump underwater, clutching my head. I let myself sink to the bottom, then push off.

The board drifts nearby, shuddering. I tread water, tasting blood in my mouth, then climb back on and paddle out.

I catch more waves. Bill never returns. Twice I ride standing up for pretty far stretches, but mostly I fall, pop up and get hit by the board again or it slams onto water beside me.

I do this until I can't do it anymore, until I'm numb from the cold, my arms ache, I'm light-headed from hunger and I don't know where, or who, I am.

———————

After school I walk to the beach. There are days when it's too cold to go in without a wet suit, but otherwise, if the waves are ridable, I run home for the board.

Waxing the deck, I look at the ocean, at any surfers already in the "lineup," the area out past the white water where the waves are caught.

With the board on the crown of my head, I pick my way across the pale domes of coral, their combs crumbling underfoot. Once I fall to my knees and the board grazes my shoulder as it crashes down.

On the verge of deeper water, I heave the board so that it glides out ahead, swim to it and climb on. Always it's as if I'm setting forth on a sea voyage. The boat-like board adds to this solemn, momentous mood. I look about warily. My fingers brush a clump of seaweed and I gasp and jerk them back. Mysterious eddies glint, coil, uncoil, vanish with a squirt. Sometimes, early in the morning or when there's no wind, an oily sheen films the water and the smell of fish hangs over it. Fins flick the surface and I race away from the spot. Once the water around me is pocked with tiny swirls and it's all I can do simply to keep dipping my hands in.

The board. It's as if no one can remember a time when such hulks were actually ridden. It's greeted with giggles, jeering. But everything gives me away: my pallor, the dullness of my hair, the Bermuda shorts I wear instead of baggies. Half the time the nose of the board plunges underwater ("pearls") as I leap to my feet, and I tumble into the drink. I've learned to wait below until I hear it strike the water. It sounds like a plank dropped on the roof of a house. Even then I surface with both hands held upward, as if in supplication.

The surfers ignore me for the most part, though I eavesdrop. "Cutback," I hear, and "head-dip." They're like gods, with their own language and sharp masterful profiles, bright hair, unerring movements. I seek only to avoid offending them.

I want to surf with Joe's older brother, Ian, but he goes out at another beach, and I can barely stagger the three blocks from Jamestown Apartments.

Swimming to shore after falling ("eating it"), when the board washes all the way in, I do a crawl, looking up at the evening sky, then back over my shoulder to be sure another surfer's board isn't washing toward me on a line of "soup" (white water).

Today Joe has come along to watch. I scan the crest of the beach for his slight, attentive silhouette. He's gone home. His parents have forbidden him to begin surfing until he's older. Not that he seems at all eager. The ocean troubles him, I can see it in his glances, hear it in the tone of his voice.

Why is my mother willing to let me risk my life when Joe's parents are not, when apparently none of the parents of boys my age let their sons surf? Doesn't she care whether I live or die?

No, she's just ignorant. I keep her that way, say nothing about how dangerous this is, how near I come to being injured by the sharp point of someone else's board or knocked unconscious by my own.

Slowly I improve, fall less frequently, learn to gauge the waves better. The Bermuda shorts are replaced by gray gym shorts, and these in turn by a pair of blue baggies, which Mom buys for me, along with bars of wax, in Ron Jon's, the famous surf shop in Cocoa Beach, where the air is fragrant with neoprene and resin and I wander wide-eyed down the long rows of flawless new boards. The fat vanishes, my skin darkens and the tips of my hair, then the rest of it, turn white blond, so that well before I can truly surf, I assume, like the chameleon, the appearance of my surroundings.

———

One morning when I tap the aquarium it doesn't stir. I reach in and pluck it from the branch: it's stiff, desiccated, the ribs visible through its grainy skin.

Panicked, I stash the corpse behind some boxes in my closet, then tell Mom that it escaped. For a week afterward, the stench is so terrible that she concludes a rat must have died in the wall, but she doesn't check the closet and I live with the smell as my punishment for having let the poor chameleon perish.

———

An older surfer paddles up. He has a long, mossy beard and the creased seafaring face of a friendly pirate. Without preamble, he lifts the nose of my board and runs a hand along the rail. "Wanna trade for something smaller?"

I don't understand. "Trade?"

"Yeah, I have a smaller board at home. I'll trade you it for this board."

"You want this thing?"

"Well, not exactly." He laughs. "I'll strip off the glass and reshape it."

We take a wave in together and walk to his house. The small garage is cluttered with cans of resin, tangled bolts of fiberglass, half-shaped foam blanks, carpenter's horses. He slides a board from among a few leaning against each other along the back wall.

"It's six foot three," he tells me. "I cut it down from a log like yours."

"Wow." I pick it up. "How'd you learn to do this?"

"You just kind of teach yourself. It's either that or pay all your dough to fuckin' Ron Jon's, you know?"

"Yeah," I say, "I know."

The fin is oddly shaped, and the decorative blue triangle defining the nose is amateurish. But at least I can carry it tucked up under my armpit.

"It's a deal!" I tell him.

"Righteous."

Now I'm able to explore, to walk half a mile, a mile, up or down the hard gleaming sand until I see surfers in the water. Sometimes the reception is unfriendly, as if they deem it necessary to protect their spots from outsiders, though I never see anything particularly distinctive about the surf.

It's not like the old pictures of Hawaii, where four or five surfers cruise blithely along together, aloha. The surf isn't like that here, and neither are the surfers. Waves usually appear quickly and must be milked for speed and length of ride. Surfers stalk them, muttering, faces drawn taut. If there is any sharing, it's unintentional or derisive, as in "This wave's not worth fighting over—let's all take it." Waves are claimed according to who's closest to the peak or up on his feet first. "My wave!" or "Coming down!" they shout to warn others away, and this claim is usually honored, though sometimes, for reasons still obscure to me, it's not. Then shouting can erupt, though other times nothing comes of the poaching and there's even laughter.

Once, dazed by a sudden swirl of action, I'm on the verge of catching a wave already claimed by another surfer. I pull back but it's too late: my board causes the wave to crumble below me, marring it. Streaking past, the surfer barks something.

I return to the lineup. The early morning sunlight is molten on the water. I'm sitting in a cave of gold.

Someone paddles up close beside me. Without looking over, I know it's the surfer whose wave I sullied.

"What the fuck was *that*?"

I gaze at the droplets scattered across the nose of my board. Am I seeing all this for the last time? Will I be struck dead?

"Hey!" he calls to someone. "This punk was about to drop in on me!"

"Who?" Utter disbelief.

"This little *kid* here!"

"Him?"

"Can you believe that shit?"

"Hey," he says, "you ever try that again, you'll wake up in the hospital!"

It's not the same as in the school yard, where I was hazed for being new. Here I'm making real mistakes and being punished, by either the waves or the surfers, sometimes by both at once. The laws are obscure and harsh, but I'm learning them.

Picking my way through the shallows at the end of the day, I feel rather than think about these things—the severity and the strange sense of hope that floats alongside and interweaves with it. I'm a day darker, a day calmer in my knowledge, but it's as if the thoughts and bits of knowledge are moving through my body, through my veins, instead of my mind.

Just before shore, I put my foot down on a skate. It flutters, sending a shock up my leg. I charge up onto the beach, where I turn and look back at the water and have to laugh: the ocean has said, "Here's one last thing to think about."

The highway is now a border between worlds. As I cross it and the red brick of the Jamestown Apartments rises into view, a heaviness comes over me.

I enter through the back gate and set the board down along the fence, rinse my feet under a spigot.

Inside, Pat is cutting meat at the dinner table. As I open the sliding-glass doors he looks up.

"Did you rinse off?"

"Yes."

"Well, do it again. You've been tracking sand everywhere."

———

I make friends with a cynical fifth-grader named Pierre. He wears his cords slung so low, the shirts tucked in, that he scuttles.

He's come with me to check the surf. It's tiny, windblown on top of it.

"It sucks."

"Yeah," I admit, but something in his tone puts me on the defensive. "It was better the other day."

"It always sucks here."

"Not always," I protest.

"Then when?"

"The day before yesterday!"

"Uh-huh." He doesn't believe me. Some people will never surf. It puzzles me.

We go to my house to listen to records. In the kitchen, getting a glass of water, I see a pack of Pat's Tareytons on the windowsill. As if in a trance, I open it and steal two.

I show them in my palm to Pierre and he leads me out the door. We stand on the lawn and scan the area, then walk along the sidewalk.

"Here," Pierre says finally. Looking around to be sure no one has seen us, we squeeze into a narrow alley between town houses.

The wind keeps blowing out the match. Pierre turns his back to the alley's exit, and we crouch down and finally get one lit and smoke a few puffs, passing it back and forth. It tastes like burnt trash.

"You're drooling on it," says Pierre, who smokes every day. When it blows out again, he says, "Fuck it."

As the front door closes behind us, Pat stalks into the foyer, face dark with intelligence and suspicion. He's wearing a dashiki, shorts and sandals. A lit cigarette is pinched between two fingers. In the other hand, his sunglasses, wedding band aglint in the gloom of the hallway.

"Did you take cigarettes from the pack in the kitchen?"

The breath goes out of me.

"No."

He knows better, of course, he knows everything, but I can no more bring myself to tell the truth than I could stay put if a big dog were bearing down on me.

"Who did?"

I shrug.

"Look, that was a brand-new pack. Did it open itself?"

"I don't know." I feel like I'm going to faint.

"You don't know. Fine." He turns as if to walk away then wheels around.

"You want to play games? We'll play games. Empty your goddamn pockets, both of you."

Pierre reaches down into the front pockets of his low-riding cords and to my amazement produces only a dime and a penny.

Hoping for the same miraculous results, I reach into mine. My hand comes up holding not only the half-smoked Tareyton but the cellophane I must have thrust in after opening the pack.

I flinch as Pat snatches it.

"Now yours, slick," he tells Pierre, who shoots me a glance then goes into his pocket again, this time tweezing the second cigarette with two fingers.

Pat snatches it.

"Now," he says, jabbing a finger at the door, "you go home!"

Pierre shrugs and puts his hand on the doorknob.

"And you can bet your ass I'm calling your parents!"

A smirk of defiance tries to form itself on Pierre's lips but wilts under Pat's glare, and he opens the door and scuttles out.

Sunlight washes briefly over Pat's face, then the door swings shut and the foyer is gloomy again, gloomier.

Pat compresses his lips, shakes his head.

"You know," he begins, gnashing the words, and then, as if disgusted at their taste, waves a hand and stalks away.

Peering under my brows, I watch him disappear around the corner into the kitchen. Could it be over? I've seen him this angry before, at Adam, who actually seems to enjoy provoking him. Yesterday morning he told Pat, "Your breath smells bad."

How it will go with me I don't know, though. I put my right foot on the first step of the staircase and tentatively, as if testing a sprained ankle, shift my weight forward to go up.

But out of the corner of my eye I see him sweeping back into the hall, like a bull released from its pen, and I step down and gaze, penitently I hope, at the parquet floor. I'm still afraid, but the pause has given me a chance to recover from the shock of being caught.

"You know!" he shouts. "You come in here—" He shakes his head, huffing from the force of his rage, grimacing. I find myself feeling a little sorry for him. He can barely get the words out.

At the same time, I take refuge in a sense of moral superiority. What, after all, have I done? Stolen cigarettes, told a little lie. Why get so worked up? I'm not an evil boy. Am I?

"You come in here!" he booms. Yes, I think, I come in here.

"You come in here," he repeats, "I ask you a simple goddamn question, and you look me dead in the eye and *lie through your goddamned teeth!*"

I pinch my thigh to keep from laughing at this, the image of God cursing my teeth.

He does a double take, cocks his head. "Is that funny?"

I frown, shake my head. Nothing could be more serious!

He switches the cigarette from right to left hand and I think he might backhand me.

"You're a *liar!*" he says. "Is that funny?"

I shake my head.

"Answer me!"

"No," I croak.

"You're goddamned right it's not!"

He pulls the pack of Tareytons from his pocket and waves it under my nose. I flinch.

"You went into my stuff! You stole! And then you had the gall to lie about it?" Spittle arcs downward from his teeth. "Think you're so damn smart!" He leans closer. "Don't you?"

I shake my head.

"You're spoiled rotten is what you are, you and your little brother both! You manipulate, you play games!"

He puts on the high-pitched voice of a boy: "Oh, hey, man, let's go rip off my stepdad's cigarettes. It's cool! Right on!"

He resumes his own voice dramatically. "Go into my stuff

behind my back then lie about it? I have news for you, mister: that shit doesn't fly with me!"

He wheels away, the muscles in his calves rippling, then comes back, bends down confidentially. "And let me give you a little advice, my friend: if you're going to lie, be sure to at least *cover your ass!*"

He stalks into the kitchen.

I wait a beat, then put my foot on the lowest step. But no, he's coming back. I remove my foot.

How many more ways are there to go over this? Oh, many more! I try clicking my mind off, but it's impossible. His shouting buffets me, flushes me out of myself and up to the surface where the meaning of his words can work. It occurs to me that it's the sound of his own voice that's sustaining his rage, that and looking at what I've done from different angles. But understanding this doesn't save me from it.

This is the model for all future eruptions, a vulcanology: I have contempt for his lack of self-control and exaggerations, yet by the time he's done, my legs ache and a kind of crust—of hatred and dullness and shame—has formed over me. When I finally climb the stairs, I half expect to hear a cracking sound as the crust is broken.

The next day I set the board down and paddle out and the first wave washes the remains of it away.

———

There's a specific beauty to rides viewed from behind. You see the crown of a head skimming along, a hand, then a shoulder blade, spray from a turn intermingling with spray from the wave, the tip of the nose of the board flashing past as some unfathomably advanced move is executed. It's like being backstage at a play. One morning I see the rear of a thin wave shattered by someone's lower back and butt as he leans into it, gives birth to himself on the glassy table of water.

But I also like watching waves when no one is riding them, a wave rolling darkly through sparkles of sunlight in deeper water, then rising as it meets the sandbar. The way, paddling up it, I glimpse the sky through the "lip" (the crest) as it launches overhead, translucent as blown glass. What are these things? Are they alive? They hiss and rumble, trounce me with what can seem like emotional violence, come near to speaking words into my ears. Every so often, I see one emit a vapor, a cloud of spray like a scarf spit from the tube, a kind of sneeze. They spin, they coil in on themselves. Waves are like snakes: banded, gem-like, cold-blooded.

And they are snake-like in their elusiveness. There are a thousand ways to miss. They slide sideways, rear up and threaten to break, then subside. They mutate abruptly, change from wall to peak and back to wall. Each is unique yet they bear family resemblances, seem to travel in clans: the Glassies, the Choppies, the Bumpies, the Barely Theres.

Finally a small, reasonable one rolls toward me. It's maintaining a single identity, posing no riddles. This should be easy, though by now I know that it won't be, that none of this is.

I turn, paddle, and when I feel it thrusting me forward, I stand up, spray in my eyes—but too soon, and I'm left behind, frozen ridiculously in place, like the statue of a conquistador.

Or the opposite: I delay rising to my feet and am sent tumbling when I finally try.

Or I paddle with great determination but it's not catchable at all, this one, I've misjudged it, and yet all my paddling has left me over the bar, in the impact zone, and the next wave proceeds to break on top of me, jerks the board from my arms with a growl and sends me swimming to shore again.

Sometimes it rains, softly, almost unnoticeably, then with ferocity, the drops pelting the slate-colored water, a million nipples leaping up, visibility contracting to a few feet. If the surf has been choppy, it becomes glassy and sleek. To be out in the ocean then is marvelous, a defiance, the wild opposite of a ruined picnic or game of baseball. But it can also rain so hard that the waves are canceled, beaten flat like lead.

Then there are the days when there are no waves to begin with. The palmettos and sea oats are motionless, and the ocean as it comes into view is like a gray window shade being lowered. At the bottom a minuscule shore break draws back, folds over and slides soundlessly up the slope.

Joe and I wander down to the water. We share an orange, spit the white seeds into the air, stroll along the beach.

It's littered with Portuguese man-of-wars, electric blue tentacles snarled on the sand. The bladders writhe and stretch, gleaming like internal organs exposed unnaturally to the light of day.

We find sharp sticks of driftwood. I twirl mine. "*En garde!*" I lunge and thrust. "Unh!"

Joe grasps his with both hands, raises it overhead. "The heart of a vampire. You are sleeping now, Dracula, but you must— die!"

Pierced, the bladders hiss or sigh or fart softly, like balloons the day after a birthday party.

"Miss Clark's face!" I thrust the stick. "Ah! Take that!"

Joe: "Her booby—uh!"

"Four times five!" I shout and stab, but nothing happens. Joe giggles. "He hasn't done his homework."

I frown, cock my head and bend down to make myself clear. "I *said,* 'Four times five!'" I thrust the stick.

A mist hits my eyes. I straighten and raise a hand helplessly toward my face. I'm wearing a blindfold of fire.

"I can't see!"

Joe giggles. "'I can't see!'"

I paw my eyes and stumble up the beach. Joe is shouting something but I'm concentrating on the pain. At the crest of the beach I crash through palmettos and wade out into A1A. The cars look like fish seen from a distance in bluish water. I'm going blind!

Joe is running alongside, speaking in gibberish.

Sobbing, I burst into the town house. Pat catches me by the elbows.

"What happened?"

Joe tells him. Pat disappears, returns with a damp washcloth, leads me out to the car by the hand. I lie down in the backseat, toss, clutch my head.

"Now don't rub it," he warns gently and then we're moving, eventually passing over the causeway bridge to Melbourne, the tires moaning across the grille of the bridge harmonizing with my moans.

In the emergency room, I'm hoisted onto a table covered by paper, my hands are forced away from my face, a penlight shined horribly into my eyes.

Someone, a doctor, says, "It didn't hit the eyes, just the lids."

Then "You're lucky."

Lashing side to side, I mutter, "Real lucky!"

Pat chuckles. "He needs something," he says.

"This should do the trick."

The pain of the shot is nothing beside the other, but before long, deliciously, neither exists. I sit up, sigh with pleasure. Pat steers me through the waiting room, the automatic doors part, we float outside.

Sun splashes the parking lot.

Lying in the backseat, I watch the sky through the rear window, breathing with the gills of light passing into the car. At the causeway, the bridge has been raised in my honor; the cormorants perched along the cables have their wings outstretched. With lordly benevolence I observe the tip of a mast skimming past.

Pat turns to check on me. "Feeling better about now, I bet, huh?"

I nod, unable to erase a small blissful smile.

How will I manage to hate him now?

Three

Close by Apollo Elementary are a baseball diamond and a warren-like palmetto field, sandy paths beaten into the interior. When the lights of the field are switched on, teenagers in flip-flops and Levi's, halter tops and bell-bottoms, trace lazy figure eights around the bleachers on Sting-Rays and ten-speeds, hang by their fingers from the wire backstop, sit cross-legged on the dusty ground in sullen powwows.

Joe and I walk to the field to try out for Little League. Heavy rain clouds are being pried open by great blades of sunshine. The clouds crack apart as we watch, the sky clears.

A coach puts the crowd of new players in alphabetical order for batting. Joe disappears into the middle of the long line and I, as always, bring up the rear. It's wearisome, this alphabetical exile.

With surfing, there's none of this: no batting orders, fences, dugouts, no coaches or clipboards. There are barely any words spoken. It's all hoots and grunts and howls. You paddle out, surf until you've surfed enough, come in. Thinking about it like this, I feel an impulse to walk away, to turn my back on organized fun.

But I crave an audience, official glory, which is what surfing lacks, at least in Indian Harbour Beach, where the shore is usually all but deserted. Though one day a beautiful woman in a bikini, brown limbs gleaming with oil, pulled her chair down near the water. I dedicated every wave to her, swimming in quickly when I lost my board, paddling back out tirelessly. She gazed devoutly in my direction. It surprised but also inspired me, and I began to reach beyond myself, to try new, difficult maneuvers. Finally the board washed up at her feet.

I kept my eyes fixed modestly on the ground. Only when I reached down for the board did I allow myself to look at her directly. Resting on the bridge of her nose was a pair of those hard plastic blinders.

A coach on the mound is calling each player to the batting box: Benson, Bryant, Burkalter, Carter. I'd like a short, clear, completely American name like Carter. Craig Carter. It would place one near the beginning of lines, but not at the very first, which is probably as bad in its way as being last.

Neither of my names is normal in the least. Those racks of personalized bicycle plates rub this in, and I've given up hope of finding Thad among them, teased by the existence of Todd and Brad, heart skipping a beat in the rare encounter of a Tad.

When the coach finally reaches Z, the sun will be dropping behind that bank of clouds above the river. He'll pause, cast about for a clue to the pronunciation of these queer, foreign syllables. "Zeeow?" he'll say. "Zow?"

"You!" It's Pierre, mock-angry. "Your stepdad got me grounded!"

"Oh. Sorry."

"That motherfucker's scary!"

"Tell me about it." Despotic parents, especially stepparents, confer prestige, so there's no advantage in telling Pierre about the emergency-room episode, how it complicated my view of Pat. It's unlikely I could put it into words even if I chose to try.

With him is a tall girl named Cherie. She's pale, covered with freckles. Her hair is long and orange-red. Pierre tells her the story.

"I palmed mine, but doofus here . . ." She rolls her eyes but gazes at me fondly, impressed with our troublemaking. They wander off.

"Later."

"Later."

The line is crawling forward. If I had Pat's name, I would have been up to bat already, out shagging fly balls in the sunlit outfield. I have his glove tucked under my arm.

I could, I suppose, take his name. The idea floats down like a leaf. He might "adopt" me. That's commonplace here. The child is absorbed like a rib into the body of the stepfather and calls him "Dad." That I would have trouble doing.

Thad Burke. It would be like starting life over in a new country. That's what this is, after all. It's like living in Brazil. We're so far from Washington that Dad need never find out. Assuming that he would care one way or the other.

As predicted, the sun is nearly down when I get to the plate, the ball a faint glow. I strike five times, six, frustrated nearly to tears, but then on the final pitch, swinging with a blind fury, I connect and the ball sails into the gloom of the deep outfield.

I find Mom in the kitchen, making dinner. Adam's coloring at the table. I tell her about the impressive hit, omitting the six strikes that led up to it, then take a breath and broach the change of name.

Adam looks up from his crayons, frowns.

"See, that way," I add, hoping to give it a whimsical inflection, "I won't always have to be last in line!"

She smiles at that then turns serious. "You don't want to change your name, honey."

"Why not?"

Adam shakes his head.

"No," she says gently. "You have a last name. It's your father's. If you change it, you'll wish you hadn't later on, when you're older."

I look at the floor.

"See what I mean?"

"Okay, yeah," I say finally. "I do."

I stare despondently at the surf. For the past five days, in what seems to me like every possible permutation, it's been unridable— lake-like flat, tiny and wind-tattered, large and ominously disorganized, medium-sized but crosshatched by what looked like several swells arriving from different directions, and now, today, both too small and too choppy.

Is this personal? Does it have anything to do with what I do, how I or anyone else behaves? Or is it no different from the weather?

I walk down to the Little League field. Pierre and Cherie are there. We lean against the right-field fence and watch a team practice. When someone bobbles a grounder or loses a fly ball in the sun, one of us calls out, "Nice one!" or "Way to go!"

Eventually Pierre spots someone in the distance, a girl. "Later."

Cherie watches. "Mystery date," she says.

As the sun sets, more kids appear, like bats flitting in the twilight. Bored of watching the practice, Cherie and I stroll around the bleachers together. Now and then the knuckles of our hands brush.

When she stops to talk to an older girl sitting cross-legged on the ground, I stand off to one side. The girl, Cherie explains in jaded tones afterward, was asking about Cherie's older sister, who has been grounded because she was caught with pills, downers.

Oh, downers, of course. I nod sagely.

What I wish is that I would also be "grounded," emerge pale and bitter days later, able then to chime in with the chorus of universal resentment, to curse my parents with cause and conviction. Pat and Mom must not believe in it, though, since even after being caught stealing the Tareytons I was allowed to come and go as I liked.

Cherie and I wander away from the crowds, the lights of the fields flooding upward behind us. Each time our hands brush, a jolt of pleasure and fear passes into me.

Something is going to happen, I feel it in my chest. Finally it does: we lace our fingers together.

A solemn, ceremonial atmosphere descends, like nuptials. Our strides synchronize, we gaze chastely at the ground. We will, it seems, be together forever, from this night forward. On the tip of her middle finger is a small wart.

We reach the entrance to one of the paths. I lead her by the hand. The palmettos come to the level of our heads then higher; the narrow path twists. Finally we emerge into a small clearing. Six other couples are sitting in a circle.

We sit down with them. It's too dark to make out their faces, though they are older, kissing or sitting with their arms draped over each other's shoulders.

One of them, a kid with hair so white-blond it glows in the dark, hands across a bottle in a paper bag. "Boone's Farm?"

We shake our heads, sit staring straight ahead, still unable to look at each other.

The surfer swigs from the bottle, observes us for a moment. "Aren't you going to kiss her?"

I shrug. I want to, but it's delicate. How can I be absolutely sure she wants me to?

"Put your arm around her," the boy suggests.

I pause, not wanting to appear to be merely following orders, then unlace my fingers from Cherie's and reach an arm stiffly over her neck and shoulders.

She leans perhaps ever so slightly against me, her long fine hair fallen forward in a curtain so that, when I turn, I can see only her nose, an eyelash.

"Now kiss her," the boy says quietly.

Again I pause for the sake of appearances then lean toward her. But I simply can't take this momentous step alone.

I lean back, look over at her. Cherie stares catatonically.

"Go on," the boy says. "She wants you to."

"Do you?" She says nothing. "Cherie?"

"What?" It's like I've woken her from a nap.

"Do you?"

"What?"

"Want me to."

She shrugs.

I lean with greater determination but again pause. Everyone in the circle is watching now.

"Just kiss her!" says a girl laughing. She rises, crosses the sand to us, presses our heads toward each other. We stiffen in resistance. She laughs, returns to her place.

A few minutes pass. My mind is blank, dull, my will broken. Despairing, I whisper to Cherie, "If you want me to, I will."

"I don't care. If you want to."

"But do you want me to?"

She shrugs. It's as if there's a gap in the air between us. When I first leaned toward her, it was narrow, negligible. But the longer I wait and the more I ask, the wider the gap grows, until she's so far away that I can't reach her and never will.

She stands up, I stay put.

"Later," she says.

"Later."

We were married, now we're divorced.

———

Late spring. Mom enrolls me in a Saturday morning painting class in Indialantic, a town three or four miles to the south. We stop at a traffic light within half a block of the boardwalk.

"Turn down there!"

She complies reluctantly. "We're going to be late."

"I just want to check it."

We drive alongside the boardwalk for a block. From here, the surf looks flat.

"No good?" she asks, glancing at it.

"No good."

But as the car turns away from the beach, something sweeps into view above the railing. A gull, a crest? I twist around to get a better look.

"It'll be there when you get home."

"Oh, I know," I say, though what I really know is that waves don't wait. They're always changing, usually for the worse.

She drops me off in front of a two-story building, then idles the car as I climb the stairs to the studio. Other than a mousy boy, the other students are women Mom's age. The teacher has long brown hair, sad eyes, a droopy mustache the color of his tooled leather vest.

He smiles at me—"Hi, I'm Michael"—and hands me a smock.

I slip it on, sit on one of the metal stools, arrange the jars of paint and pick up a brush. At the center of the room is a still life of wood boxes and drapery. I try to see in its utter dullness a challenge to my talent, an occasion to which I will rise.

I've never painted like this, but since I consider myself good at drawing, I'm prepared to produce a masterpiece on the first try. Why not? I have a vision of it gleaming like a photograph on the easel, so breathtakingly good that the teacher staggers dumbstruck before it, the ladies gather around, Mom has it framed and sent special delivery to Dad, who hangs it in his office.

The only lessons I've had, if that's the word, were given to me in D.C. by an artist named Charles, a hippie to whose apartment my parents sent me. "Draw me," he would say, "but quick. Thirty seconds each." So, while he ate an orange or spoke on the phone, I sketched. "Artists don't erase," he warned me, "they correct." That seemed to exhaust his stock of wisdom.

The teacher begins to move from easel to easel. I inspect what I've painted so far: a pink square, a blue square, the edge of the brown table underneath. It doesn't look like a photograph, it looks like dried toothpaste.

"There's a hint of blue in that shadow," the teacher's saying to someone. "See it? The violet?"

This gives me an idea. The sunlight flooding the studio looks like banana mashed up in milk. I mix an approximation of this color and spread it around the boxes of the still life. If it can't be photographic, it can always be "abstract."

Palm fronds rasp against the louvered windows, curled tips feeling into the studio. The teacher arrives behind my shoulder.

"I need to use the bathroom," I tell him.

He's peering at my easel with undisguised perplexity.

"Down the hall to the left," he says finally.

I peel off the smock and leave it on my stool. Out in the hall, instead of finding the bathroom, I go down to stand in the sun for a minute.

The two lanes of traffic headed toward the boardwalk crawl forward, sunlight erupting on the chrome, rock music leaking into the air through the open windows. Occasionally there are boards strapped to the roofs on racks.

I glance up the staircase then turn and jog toward the board-walk. I pass a pharmacy, a bank, gift shops. At the main intersection there's a van with an intricate airbrushed Eden: flowering vines, green jungle leaves, a blue snake, the eyes of various animals peering out, the central pair of which seem to be turning into a woman's.

Crowds seethe between cars alongside A1A. There is the sound of conga drums in the distance. It reminds me of Dupont Circle, though the hippies here are blonder and nuder. And the black people are missing.

I scan the buildings for Darcy's, the surf shop owned by the famous Phil Meta, see its sign and go in.

A fat man is reading a newspaper spread out across the top of a glass display case filled with pot pipes, rolling papers, silver roach clips.

"Is this Darcy's?"

Without looking up, he points to a door at the back. I go through it and into a small room lit by black lights, the posters on display seeming to float, to throb milkily. I pause in front of one called Your Zodiac Signs.

Streaming with Day-Glo colors, a man and woman are having sex in more positions than I would have thought possible. I search hastily for the Aquarian position, discovering to my vague unease that it's doggy style, the woman on all fours, the man behind her. Who's the Aquarian here, the man or the woman? Or are they both Aquarians?

I go through another door and into a sunlit room. Here there are racks of boards, surf posters, framed photographs.

In the front room, a tall broad-shouldered man with short sandy hair leans against the cash register counter, arms folded across his chest.

A pair of surfers comes in.

"What's going on, Phil?"

Meta says, "What's going on? Have you guys checked it yet?"

Their eyes widen, and they shake their heads and begin to back out of the doorway.

"I'm just waiting for someone to come take over!" Meta calls after them. "That's how good it is!"

As if he's noted me hovering in the background all along, Meta turns the grin on me. "What about you there?"

"Guess I should go, too!" I tell him.

"This is no day to be indoors, kid!"

I scamper past him and out the door to the street. I dart through the crowd, hop up onto the boardwalk, grab the railing with both hands and gasp.

A set of large glassy waves, animate hill country, is rolling through dense knots of surfers, more people on boards than I've seen in one spot, their backs gleaming in the sun, boards glinting, the water a blue-green that makes my heart ache with longing. Still more surfers are picking their way down the sand.

The last wave of the set is the largest. Out of the swarm, perhaps ten paddle seriously to catch it, crossing each other's paths, doubling back, kicking, splashing more and more frantically as the wave rises and feathers, spreads out before the boardwalk like a billboard. People around me put up a hand against the glare.

Of these contenders, only two catch the peak, and one of them, as if unwilling to encroach upon the other, makes a quick turn at the top and kicks out, leaping for his board as it begins to spin in the back draft and clasping it to his chest with both arms, then falling from view over the wave's back.

The second surfer, victor, hero, hair slicked back in the shape of a helmet, executes a smooth bottom turn, the board a flat knife in icing, then floats back to the top.

There he pauses, sighting down his arm. Everyone on the beach and everyone in the water, in the world, it seems to me, is watching now. A thick meringue of foam carpets the water in front of the wave, a fine clean spray twinkles in the air. Led Zeppelin's "Communication Breakdown" on the tinny portable radios is the soundtrack, the fragrance of coconut suntan lotion the atmosphere, the oxygen.

How I wish I could fly out through the air and take over! The wave is huge and steep, but from where the surfer's positioned himself on it now, I could ride it, I could! It gleams like the skin of a dolphin and has stretched out so far down the beach before him that I wouldn't be surprised if it went on forever.

———

I pace in front of the studio like a deranged zoo animal. When Mom finally arrives, I tell her I have no interest in going back. She seems to have expected as much.

The swell lasts for three days and on the last morning I'm in pain, aflame with wax rash and badly sunburned—not only my skin but my eyes too, somehow.

"One more wave," I think, but that's what I've been telling myself for over an hour.

The sun on the water is like a sheet of foil, the others spidery black figures against it. I can't look at it directly; my eyes roll away. I stop paddling and sit up. The film of seawater running down my stomach is striated with blood from my chafed nipples.

That night my eyes sting and water when I close them, and hot tears spill down my cheeks and neck. I twist and sweat in the sheets, moan loudly instead of actually calling for Mom, who eventually appears in the doorway with a glass of water and aspirin, folds a damp washcloth over my eyes. In the morning she takes me to a doctor.

A brusque man with a withered, flabby neck and hooded eyes, he reminds me of a fence lizard. He tilts my head back roughly, peels back the lids of my eyes. I let him peer into them through his device for a few seconds then, eyes tearing painfully, jerk my head away.

"Easy, boy," he warns in a low voice. I feel an urge to strike him.

"What he's got is a kind of snow blindness, except of course he got it from the glare off the water."

"What should we do for it?"

He shrugs. "Stay out of the water until they clear up." He makes it sound easy. "Meanwhile, get him to wear a pair of sunglasses, dark ones."

"What if I wore sunglasses in the water?"

He chuckles dryly. "You could, I guess. If you can keep 'em on."

———

I sometimes run into Bill, Long Hair of my first morning in the waves. He's nineteen and lives with his parents in Jamestown Apartments. Today I find him cleaning out the back of his red van in a corner of the parking lot.

"Nice shades," he says.

I describe my tragic condition.

"Hey, it could be worse. Bloodshot eyes? That's a great cover."

"For what?"

"For what." He looks me up and down, reassessing. Behind him, Debbie, a beautiful blonde, is approaching across the lot, wearing, as usual, a yellow bikini.

"You've never gotten high, have you?"

"No," I admit.

"Interested?"

"Sure," I say with a shrug, more flattered than curious—then more nervous than flattered. I've seen pot before, set out loose in a wooden bowl before a party at our house—in D.C., that is, before the divorce. There's been no sign of it since Pat's arrival. But I often see people, surfers, non-surfers, kids not much older than myself, silhouetted in the evening at the baseball field or early in the morning before surfing, passing joints, and catch whiffs of it on the humid breeze.

Debbie saunters up.

"The kid here," Bill tells her, "wants to get high with us."

She raises her pretty eyebrows. Blowing past overhead, puffs of cloud form a shifting leopard pattern on the lot. I feel high already.

"Have you ever smoked before?" she asks.

"No."

"Neither have I."

So Debbie and I are pot virgins. I'm thinking of the talk Mom had with me about sex the other night, including slang like "to pop her cherry." Pat was moving about within earshot throughout, and I was too embarrassed to retain much beyond the sense that she seemed to believe me to be on the threshold of depravity.

Bill's disappeared, then his head pokes clownishly from the door of one of the empty carports. He looks both ways and waves us over. We find him squatting against one stucco wall, the joint already pinched between thumb and first finger. Debbie sits beside him and I sit across from them on the gritty concrete floor.

Bill lights the joint with a silver lighter, inhales lengthily, elbow cocked, then passes it to Debbie, who peers at it, draws delicately, holds it for two beats then coughs up the smoke, at which Bill laughs, half honk, half machine gun.

Debbie slugs him in the arm, then gets up and passes it to me. Our fingers brush. Sea salt has dried in the down on her tanned breasts. I catch a glimpse of the pink of one of her nipples then look at the joint—a burning twist of paper, exactly like the magazine photos. I can't hold in the smoke very long either.

It's passed around again, then once more, then once again. I don't feel a thing.

Debbie says, "Say something."

"Something," says Bill, and honks.

"I like it," I say.

"Hey, how old are you anyway?" Bill says.

"Ten."

"God."

"You look older than ten," Debbie says. I blush with pleasure: the desire to appear older than you are informs everything.

"No shit," says Bill. "I thought he was at least twelve." He honks again.

A leaning trunk of sunlight appears in the doorway of the garage then vanishes.

I gaze dreamily at the floor. "I see butterflies." As I say it I do see them, sort of, floating stylized and transparent, though they bear a suspicious resemblance to a certain surfboard logo.

"You don't hallucinate on pot," says Bill sternly, "man."

Debbie glances from me to Bill. "You don't know, Bill. Maybe some people do."

The air smells of rain. A car cruises past outside, bringing Pat to mind.

"I better get going," I tell them. "Thanks, Bill."

"Don't forget your shades, Stevie Wonder."

In a kitchen drawer I find long rubber bands. I tie them together, then to the stems of my sunglasses, and put them on. The rubber grabs my hair painfully.

It's been over a week since the visit to the doctor. My eyes are still bloodshot.

Mom laughs. "You look like you need a cane instead of a surfboard."

"But they'll stay on."

She turns serious. "I hope so, because you really will be blind if you keep this up."

I carry the board out to the car and slide it nose-first through the sunroof of the Volkswagen. She's going to drop me at the boardwalk. School has let out and it's hotter, brighter, more humid. This full-bodied, all-engulfing heat is what I expected from Florida, and I relish it, even the steam bath of the car, the vinyl seat sticky against my bare back.

As she pulls out onto A1A, Mom asks why my grades are so mediocre and what I might do next year to improve them, but neither of us much cares, and after replying absentmindedly I concentrate on trying to catch a glimpse of the surf.

Near the boardwalk traffic slows and the crowds of beach hippies and surfers mill about, thicker now that summer's arrived, a montage of feverishly strummed acoustic guitars, dogs on rope leashes, a spider monkey scaling an outstretched arm, halter tops on slouched shoulders, blue jeans worn so low that pubic hair is visible.

From the doorway of Darcy's, wearing baggies and T-shirt and flip-flops, Phil Meta surveys the scene with a satisfied expression.

"That's Phil Meta." I wave as I say this, and to my delight Meta waves back, enfolds me briefly in his legend.

"Do you know him?" She sounds slightly alarmed.

"Sort of. Everyone does."

Looking for a place to pull over, she stares at a short, muscular teenager. He has blue greasepaint stars on his face and is gesticulating toward something invisible in the air.

"Do you think he's on speed?"

"I don't know."

"The way he's jumping around—"

"Mom, this is good—just stop here!"

She pulls the car over. "Now if someone offers you drugs, what do you do?"

"I say 'No thank you.'"

"I'm not playing. You don't say anything. You just walk away."

"I just walk away," I repeat woodenly, as if learning it by rote: "In 1492 . . ." I open the door to get out.

"Let me see your eyes." I sigh with impatience, knees jiggling, lean toward her, lower the sunglasses. "Honey, they're still so bloodshot!"

"That's because I'm high on drugs."

She grabs my face so that my cheeks bunch up and my mouth pops open. "My friend, you are one hell of a lot less sophisticated than you think!"

"My friend"—a Pat-ism. Has the man possessed her body?

I take hold of her wrist and jerk myself free. But as I do, I glimpse in her eyes the source of all this: a dark undertow flowing beneath the bright air of the boardwalk. She's afraid for me and has reason to be.

It's a passing intuition. I slouch in my seat and pout.

"I'll be back to get you at three," she says to the windshield. "Meet me right here."

I lurch out of the car, the suddenness and sunlight causing me to sway dizzily. I slam the door, slide the board out through the sunroof and stand it in the street as the car moves off.

Then I climb onto the raw wood planks of the boardwalk, into the miasma of Coppertone suntan oil, hot sea breeze and Blood, Sweat & Tears' "Spinning Wheel" as played through half a dozen cheap transistorized speakers, a kind of lethe in which my mother and all else beyond this place are forgotten.

For here I finally stand, boy warrior with his spear.

I lean the board against the railing beside three girls and, studiously ignoring them, scan the ocean. The surf is pretty good, three to four feet, still glassy and as gloriously crowded as the beach.

"Nice shades, man," says one of the girls.

I echo the sarcastic tone: "Oh, thanks."

"He looks like a chick!" stage-whispers another.

"Gidget!" says the other.

"Hey, what's with the rubber bands?"

I thought they would never ask. "It's because of this." I lower the sunglasses as if pulling aside a bandage.

"Oh my God!"

"The doctor says it's some kind of glare blindness."

They gather around.

"You," the eldest declares, holding my arm for support, "look so high it's not even funny." She's sucking on a slab of watermelon candy. I feel my breathing tighten.

"I know," I say wearily. "My mom thinks I'm stoned all the time."

"No shit."

"Anyway, if I want to surf, I have to wear the glasses."

"So, Joe Surf," she says, pulling back, "you here for the contest?"

She raises her chin toward a row of lifeguard chairs down the beach, strings of triangular white flags. Surfers wearing different-colored jerseys mill in the shade of a large square tent.

When I look back the girls are gone, weaving through the crowd.

An air horn drones and the surfers break in a phalanx from the shade of the tent and trot down the beach, gradually quickening their pace on the way, so that by the time they reach the shallows they're able to launch into the water on their outstretched boards and, backs arched, blast through the first small waves of the shore break.

I slip my board under the railing, standing it nose-down in the sand, then hop to the sand, drag the board a few feet farther down the beach and fall to my knees beside it. Glancing up now and then for the girls, I rub a bar of wax across the deck.

When I finish I look seaward, cupping my hands beside my eyes. Even with the sunglasses, it's a little painful to gaze at the water.

One of the surfers in the contest has caught a wave. A wing of spray spreads in the air above the crest.

I pick up the board and jog down the beach, weaving among

sunbathers, girls in bikinis, tourists in floppy canvas hats, toddlers smeared with oil. A puppy lunges at my ankles.

The eyes of the entire beach are upon me now, I imagine. I'm a surprise entrant in the contest. And yet there is an uncanny certainty among the judges and in the crowd that this boy is going to win. What's with the sunglasses? they ask. He has a terrible eye condition! one of the girls tells them.

"Blue baggies!"

I stop, aghast, and look back at the lifeguard stand.

A man with a megaphone to his mouth says, "Yes, you! Move down past the flags!"

A surfer jogging along the waterline waves to me and I fall in beside him. He's in his late teens.

"Oh, yeah!" he sneers, flinging an arm backward. "This whole part of the ocean's reserved strictly for surf stars!"

When we've jogged past the flag, he turns and dashes into the water and I follow. The first wave snatches the sunglasses from my face and I grimace in the light but let them dangle from my neck for now.

It's so crowded, with surfers on the same wave, and boards washing in as well, bouncing wildly or sweeping along sideways like push brooms, that I have to speed up my usual calculations, paddle frantically this way and that.

When I reach the lineup, I sit up and replace the sunglasses. The mood of the crowd is serious. No one seems to know anyone else, though I'm occasionally smiled upon.

"I love your music, Ray Charles!" says a man as he paddles around me.

I content myself with small undesirable waves and the tail end of set waves left riderless after a wipeout. The waves and the specific, spontaneous decisions I make during rides—all this is both accrued in my body as a kind of knowledge and instantly lost and erased.

When the sun looks to be nearing three o'clock, I ask a surfer with a watch for the time.

"Two forty-five."

Tired now, I sit up and idly watch a wave and rider pass by. He must have wiped out: the narrow board has shot up into the air. It corkscrews slowly, green against the blue sky.

It's too late: I roll off my board and dive under, but the board strikes the back of my head with a clank, fiberglass against skull.

When I surface, the sunglasses hang from my neck again. I see my board wheeling in a patch of foam, swim to it and hoist my elbows onto the deck.

"You all right?" The surfer who wiped out has swum up beside me.

"I think so."

He swims alongside while I paddle mechanically toward shore, then I catch a line of soup, leaving him behind. I have a headache now. In the shallows I pick up my board and start up the slope through the sunbathers. The tide has gone out; the beach is wide and hard.

A woman stares at me intently then rises from her towel and places a hand on my shoulder.

"Did you know," she says apologetically, "that your head is bleeding?"

"It is?"

"We should find a— Hey!" she yells. "He's hurt!"

"Is it that bad?" In her sunglasses I see myself, forehead wrinkled anxiously.

She peers again at the back of my head, looks queasy. "It's pretty bad."

A lifeguard, whistle dangling, appears against the wall of sunlight, nose and cheekbones smeared with zinc oxide.

"Let's have a look there." He takes my head in his hands, tenderly moves locks of hair aside.

I notice blood, thinned out in a solution of seawater, making its way down the side of my stomach and soaking into the waistband of my baggies.

"Oh, yeah," the lifeguard concludes, "you might need a stitch or two."

Someone slides my board out from under my arm and carries it for me. The lifeguard takes one elbow, the blond woman walking alongside. They guide me up the beach, past people who bring hands to their lips, point.

I'm boosted onto the boardwalk.

Mom is standing at the railing ten feet away, scanning the water.

"Wait, there's my mom. Mom!"

She starts toward us, her face filling with alarm as she grasps the meaning of the lifeguard, the blood that's begun to drip onto my shoulder.

This is what I've been keeping from her.

———————

While five stitches bind the wound, I read *Surfer* and *Surfing* and listen to a Led Zeppelin forty-five, "Immigrant Song." Rising from bed to start the record over, I hear a commotion down the hall: Adam.

"You most certainly may not!" Mom tells him, then comes the slamming of a door and, after a pause, Pat's heavy footfall on the stairs, the remonstrative rumble of his voice, which is, as always, though no less incredibly, met by the high but equally fierce sound of Adam talking back.

"You're not my dad!"

I turn up the music then flop onto the bed and return to an article about a thirteen-year-old big-wave prodigy named Jackie Dunn. He wears his trunks underneath his school clothes to save time getting into the water. His mother agreed to move to Hawaii because in California Jackie "always had a cold, so it was either pneumonia, give up surfing, or move."

There is, first of all, the perfection of his name, which brings to mind Peter Pan: Jackie—light, bright, impossible to misunderstand; Dunn—solemn and simple. Then there is his blessed mother, moving to Hawaii so he won't catch cold. Mom would do the same for me.

I gaze at the photos of Jackie, an elfin boy with white-blond hair. His chin is up and he's smiling and in his eyes burns the clean fire of stoke. I look more or less like that.

Across from these portraits is a full-page shot of him poised at the top of a large feathering wave, arms spread in a V like a tightrope walker. I don't surf like that, though I might if we lived in Hawaii.

I think a lot about Hawaii. It's hard not to: photos of its waves fill the magazines.

During the final week of school, a girl named Beverly Chang gave an oral report about Hawaii, where she had lived until this year. She spoke wistfully of the pineapple and sugarcane fields, volcanos and red clay, the "world-famous surfing." It was as though she'd fallen from heaven. At the end she passed out pieces of sugarcane.

It was ambrosial.

———

Halfway through summer, Mom announces at the dinner table that they've have found a new house in South Melbourne Beach, that we'll be moving.

I frown. "Why?"

"You," she assures me, "are gonna love it. The house—"

"I like it here—"

"Don't interrupt your mother," Pat tells me.

Adam, for whom the new is always better than the old, sits bolt upright and wide-eyed in his chair. "When do we move?"

"Settle down," Pat says. "Next month."

"The house," Mom continues, "is a block from the ocean, the river is two blocks away in the other direction, there are woods everywhere, and it's right next to Sebastian Inlet."

I shake my head.

Pat sets down his knife and fork. "What's the problem?"

"I just . . ."

"You just what?"

I don't want to leave the friends I've made, I don't want to be uprooted again.

I smirk, shake my head. "Can I be excused?"

"That's a good question," he says.

The next day, we drive thirty or so miles south along A1A to look at the house and sign the lease. There are different municipalities up and down the coast, but it's really like a single beach town, the shell shops and strip malls along the highway, the white roofs of the houses behind.

All of which ends in South Melbourne Beach, the "town" we'll be living in. Here there is only the highway running in a straight line alongside the ocean, palmetto and scrub oak, the occasional trailer on cinder blocks, a few streets leading due west to the Indian River.

Pat turns onto Surf Road, a street of ten or twelve small houses tucked into the shade of oaks, pickup trucks and small boats in the driveways, garage doors pulled down tight. The road slopes gradually and seems to vanish below sea level into the molten silver of the Indian River in the distance.

Pat pulls up to a small, sun-pounded house. The treeless crabgrass lawn is thick with sandspurs, its rear border defined by a wall of dense dry jungle. We walk up a cracked sidewalk to the front door. It's so swollen with humidity that Pat has to brace one foot on the jam and pull hard. Droplets of sweat fall from the tip of his nose.

"God—damn it!"

The door gives and he stumbles backward comically, glaring at Adam and me. Inside it's gloomy, but the lacy sparkle of a screened-in pool is visible in back, and after we glance into the rooms that will be ours, Adam and I go out through the sliding-glass doors to inspect it.

"Have a swim!" Mom says.

I'm lifting the lid of a filter to see whether a snake or frog has been trapped inside—an old habit. "We didn't bring our baggies," I tell her.

"So skinny-dip!"

The prospect of being seen naked by Pat makes me uncomfortable and I hesitate. Not Tarzan. He's already torn off his shirt and is trying to yank his pants over his tennis shoes.

"Take your shoes off first, honey."

Adam leaps, belly flops joyfully. It's so hot that I'll seem prim if I don't follow him. Keeping my eyes on the deck, I undress quickly and dive in.

While Mom snaps pictures of Adam lolling like a hairless *Playboy* model on a blow-up raft, I pretend I've wiped out in a big wave at Sunset Beach, Oahu, that I'm Jackie Dunn. I swim underwater, spiraling, pushing off the walls, coming up only when I run out of air.

———

A few days before we move, a hurricane passes up the coast, and the ocean leaps from dead flat to a size I have no way of gauging. I'm at Patrick Air Force Base with two brothers, Mark and Brian. It's just after dawn.

"Where is it?" I ask Brian. I have to raise my voice to make myself heard above the din of the ocean.

"What?" He's seventeen and angry, his forehead creased with it.

"The hurricane." I imagine it like a colossal blender, vast blades churning in the sky behind the bank of clouds on the horizon.

Brian waves an arm to the north. "Veering off toward Bermuda."

Then he hops over the seawall. Mark and I follow, sinking to our shins in the swampy sand.

The shore break alone is bigger than anything I've been out in. Now and then, objects—lumber? dead surfers?—are pitched into the air. The beach is littered with plastic bottles, torn nets, shattered paneling, buoys. A sealed can of house paint rolls down the slope.

Mark and Brian plunge in.

I pause then run my board into the water, paddle through a line of soup, then another, ready at any second, now that my hair is wet, to turn back. All I really have in mind is saving face with an attempt at getting out.

But now I'm swept forward as if towed by a rope, the water like rapids. Spray from a tube blinds me, and when my eyes clear I'm past the shore break.

I sit up on my board and peer around with big eyes. The dawn light falls on the water like a film of blood, as if a shipwreck or shark attack had taken place.

"Whoo!"

Twenty yards closer to shore, Brian is giving his curls a shake.

Relieved, I hoot back and sit up to wait for him. But he's paddling with telltale desperation. I swing around.

A wall of water is sweeping toward us, scrawled with foam as if bearing forward some urgent message from the deep. As its shadow falls across me, I think to ditch my board and swim for the bottom, anything to avoid moving farther out into this ocean, but some instinct prevents it, and as the wave heaves forward I windmill over the top.

Behind it is another, and behind that yet another—a step-ladder of three, four, five waves. My fingers claw through the shag carpet of foam until the board has gained so much momentum that it launches into the air across the ramp of the last crest, yaws to one side in a cloud of spume and pitches me into the water like a dead pilot.

I plummet through a cacophonous gurgling fizz, fight to the top and gasp in relief: the board is ten feet away, spinning slowly. I swim for it, climb on and look seaward: more waves, the biggest yet, their faces blooming with boils the size of beach towels. I paddle over them in a kind of shock.

Spray from the last one blows my hair forward in a gust. The beach is a sliver of white obscured by roiling spray. Oh, God, I've never been out so far.

Past the nose of my board drifts a chunk of tar, a white deck shoe.

Thirty yards out, a manta ray, black against the red sky, soars upward, whip-like tail dangling, white underbelly and curled wings dripping a ragged curtain of seawater. Before the splash has settled, I've wheeled around and started toward shore.

Focusing on it, I paddle. I begin to wonder whether I might make it all the way in unscathed when the grain of the water seems to pause, reverse itself, flow outward.

A wave has gathered me up. Not daring to look back, I gulp air, hug the board and squeeze my eyes shut.

Hurled forward, I float then hit the trough. The wind goes out of me with a whoosh, I bounce into the air then flop down on the board, hug it, then bounce again as the crest detonates.

My eyes clear. The shore is racing toward me. I catch a glimpse of Brian and Mark paddling side by side, disappearing headfirst into the very white water I'm being driven before. Finally, racing into the shore break, I feel the fin scrape bottom.

A pair of beachcombers in yellow rain slickers gape at me as though I've washed up clinging to a spar.

The man cups his hands by his mouth. "Are you all right?"

I try to push myself up off the deck of the board. My entire body is trembling.

A group of surfers breaks through the mist behind the beachcombers and gallop down the beach like runaway horses, centaurs.

"Whoo!" they yell.

"Oh!"

"Awoo!"

Boards held high, they sprint into the water close by, as oblivious to me as if I had drowned and become a ghost, and pitch themselves happily in.

Four

I leave the new house early, before I can be conscripted into unpacking boxes. Sunlight is just catching fire in the highest oak leaves. Down Surf Road I carry the board, across a silent A1A; the road material is crushed shells.

In the breach of a wall of sea grapes, I stand on the low crest of the beach. The surf looks fairly good, though there's no one out.

In fact, there's no one in sight. It's as if I'm Charlton Heston in the final scene of *Planet of the Apes*. Like I'm the last, or first, surfer on earth.

I set the board in the shore break. There's no coral to scrape my feet on, at least, and the water is clearer than in Indian Harbour Beach, Caribbean clear. Even in the lineup (but with whom am I lining up?), shreds of seaweed are visible washing to and fro on the sand bottom, the silver gleam of a fish rolling on its side.

Paddling out a few days later, I see a five-foot shark swimming along sideways in a wave, as clearly as if it were in an aquarium at Sea World. I snatch my hands and feet up out of the water—like the ocean has shouted, "Stick 'em up!"—and float there, breathless.

It's pale green, with long evil teeth tangled like thorns around the mouth. But the stately way it's moving, and being able to see all of it, keeps terror at bay. To see only a dorsal fin or a big thrashing in a school of fish is worse.

The wave lifts the shark then glides past, and I dip my hands, turn the board and paddle.

I miss the wave, but the beach is close. There's the striped shirt I left on the sand. This patch of deeper water between the outside bar and the shore break is spooky, though. It's calm because it's a trough, a trench—perfect for a shark.

I imagine it turning to follow the vibrations emitted by my paddling. They can swim so fast—a few sweeps of that long tail and it could be right behind me, where my feet hang over the end of the board. Who's to say it's not surging up behind me right now, inches away, wondering whether to give me a bump or just go ahead and *take a bite.*

My eyes go wide, panic surging from my toes to my fingertips. I claw the water, windmilling my arms, and the board shoots into the shore break, where a dumping wave picks me up from behind. The board pearls, squirts backward between my legs, flips forward with the crest of the wave and hits me on the back of the head.

I barely notice. I'm high-stepping out of the shallows as if the water were electrocuting me.

I keep going up the beach then whirl and scan the surf.

Adam, who's been catching sand fleas and putting them in a plastic pail, runs up. "What?"

"A shark, I saw a shark out there!"

He drops the pail. "Where? Where?"

"In a wave, right out there!" My knees are shaking.

"I don't see it!"

"Shut up! Neither do I now!"

I wrap my arms around myself and we walk south, the direction it was headed. Finally I spot it, a quivering shadow. I grab Adam's arm. "There!"

"Where?"

"On the other side of that wave!"

"Yes!"

It's scarier as a shadow. It's revealed once more inside a wave, like an afterimage, then disappears.

"Don't tell Mom. She might not let me surf out here again."

I make him promise. "I swear," he says.

But do I want to surf out here again? Even on the sunniest day, when the waves are fine and friendly, to be out alone can be eerie. I peer at my feet. Tanned on top, wrinkled and white on the bottoms, they dangle like morsels of bait. A boil in the wake of a wave, upwhirl of current, scatter of minnows, thrashing tarpon, a cloud passing across the sun—any of these can spook me into paddling for shore.

Undiluted by the presence of other people, the ocean itself threatens to overwhelm me. It moves, breathes, changes temperatures and colors, stretches out to the horizon and drops away into a strip of navy blue, where a colossal cloud explodes upward like a nuclear blast.

So I'm relieved when the surf goes flat. I wander around in the scrubby woods, most of which is impenetrably dense. It's August. There is the ever-present grind of cicadas, the rustle of a blue-tailed skink darting for cover, what turns out to be a foraging robin. The last time I was alone in the woods, in Alabama, I saw a hummingbird near the bottom branches of a tree and stood without breathing until it vanished. It was like seeing a tiny god.

I come to a man-made clearing at the crest of a low hill. There are tracks in the sand: bulldozer, raccoon, dog, land crab, deer. I follow those of the deer to a braided trickle of a creek, which leads to the river. Hoping to see a snake, I crouch on the bank among the mangrove trees, the green water lapping at their barnacle-encrusted roots.

A needlefish noses into the shallows, a colony of fiddler crabs clicks into life down the bank. Then, flying low across the water, a horsefly arrives and chases me off. I circle back to A1A and then Surf Road.

There's Pat at the bottom of the driveway, bent over the lawn mower that came with the house. He jerks the cord but it won't start.

I walk ever so quietly, but some instinct makes him look up and over his shoulder, huffing for breath.

"Hey, Nature Boy!"

I close my eyes and stop.

"How about some help?"

On my first halfhearted pull, the engine roars.

Pat gestures at the lawn. "Go to it."

I've never mowed one, if this matted stuff qualifies. Sand-spurs spray out from the vent, blanket my shoes and pants and socks. I lose track of what I've cut, grow bored, mow in straight lines, in circles, backtrack. Finally I stop. It looks done to me. I shut off the engine.

In the garage Pat's disassembling an edger.

"All done?"

I nod.

He comes out onto the driveway. "What about that?"

"Where?"

"And over there."

"By the curb?"

"Yes, by the goddamn curb!"

"I thought I got that."

He jerks the mower's cord. It won't start again. He looks up at me, red-faced. "You really are Polish, aren't you?"

My face flushes and I clench my fists, turn on my heel and stalk blindly around to the back of the house and across the yard until I reach the wall of scrub oak and vines, where I stare furiously into the dark growth.

I'll hitchhike back to Indialantic and live under the boardwalk! I'll eat out of garbage cans, behind houses; they'll never see me again.

As if hearing my thoughts, the cicadas fall silent.

I cock my head. Something is crashing through the brush, breaking up the deeply pleasing image of a bereft Mom weeping with anguish.

What a racket. It must be big enough not to care about the noise—a raccoon, a wild boar. No, bigger: panther, bear—bigger than a bear maybe.

Bigfoot!

The crashing gets closer, louder. It's not only headed this way, it's coming directly at me!

I take a step back, eyes wide, mouth open, wishing I had a knife or at least a stick. It's almost to the edge now but I can't see it yet. I get ready to run.

A football-sized armadillo waddles past my feet into the yard. I jump back, giggle with relief. Some Bigfoot.

I squint into the thicket to make sure that it's not fleeing before some other beast, but it's quiet now. The cicadas resume. Show's over.

The armadillo roots in the grass. I sneak up and grab its shell, which is warm and smooth, with bristly hairs poking up through the cracks. It grunts, bucks my hand off and scuttles across the yard then into the scrub.

From the kitchen window, Mom sees it every day at about three o'clock, on its rounds.

"Thad!" she shouts. "It's back there!"

Eventually I catch it with a dip net and pen it in the screen porch. It circles the pool, leans over the edge to sniff the water and falls in.

I fish it out with the net. It sneezes, looking sad. I place my hand on its shell.

I use the pool only to rinse off after surfing. When I went skinny-dipping the day we came to look at the house, I felt pink and hairless in front of Pat, like a girl.

I can't help it: I still don't like him. I don't like his dark hair, or his sideburns. I don't like his squint. I don't like the way he gobbles chunks of hot food or the way he pinches his Tareytons between his fingers or the way he breathes loudly through his nose. And when he yells at me for things like not pressing the sponge hard enough when I wipe the kitchen counters or losing his precious snatch hooks in the canal when I try to snag mullets, I loathe him. I go to my room, sit on the bed and seethe, like a dark building burning slowly.

I try hard to hold on to this feeling, but it leaks gradually away, and the next day or the day after when he walks to the canal at the end of the street with fishing rods and a bucket of shrimp, I end up going along. We come back at dusk with a stringer of speckled trout and flounder, and cleaning them on a trencher in the backyard, Pat can seem happy—happier, at least, than I've ever seen him.

The kitchen window is open. Adam's telling Mom something in a whisper. The armadillo has tipped over again. This is too sad. I set it on its feet and guide it out the screen door.

Watching it trundle across the yard toward the woods, I hear Adam's voice rising: "It was ten feet long and it was riding along in the waves! *In the waves,* Mom!"

———

During the last week of August, Dad flies down from D.C. It's been a long time since we've seen him, and a welter of emotions rises within me: sullen indifference, happiness, anger.

I slide my board into the Volkswagen through the sunroof and Mom drives Adam and me a few miles up A1A to the motel where he's staying. Puffs of white cloud drift in from the ocean. Adam's bouncing in the backseat.

Dad emerges from one of the rooms as we pull up and I think: "This is what I look like. This is my skin and nose and body."

"Dad!" Adam shouts. "Dad!"

He sees us, smiles, waves happily. He's wearing a white T-shirt, flip-flops and embarrassing red nut-hugger trunks with a white racing stripe on the sides, though somehow they look okay on him.

Adam bolts from the car and hurls himself headfirst into his stomach.

"Ugh!" he says. "Adam!"

I walk up and hug him over Adam. "And Thad! Such white hair on the two of you!"

"Hi, John," Mom says. They hug too. "It's good to see you."

"They're turning into real beach bunnies down here!"

"We hardly see them on land anymore."

Adam looks up. "How long you staying, Dad?"

"Just a few days this time, I'm afraid."

I say, "Do you wanna go surfing? I brought my board."

"I see that. Sure."

Adam tugs his hand. "Just a few days, Dad?"

"Thad's getting pretty good on that surfboard," Mom tells him.

Adam shouts, "I can surf too, Dad!"

I shake my head discreetly but Adam sees it and he lowers his head and flails his fists at me. "I can, too!"

I catch him by the wrists. "Okay, okay! You can!" I wink at Dad.

We drive to the beach at Surf Road, Dad following in his rental car. As usual, it's deserted. I show him how I wax the board and explain about traction, paddling, pearling, the laws of claiming a wave for one's own.

He looks up and down the beach. "It doesn't look like you have to worry about claiming a wave here. Do you surf here all by yourself?"

I shrug. "Sure."

Adam says, "We saw a shark!"

"A shark? Yikes!"

Adam squints at the water, points with his finger up by one eye. "Right . . . *there!*"

"It was just a sand shark, I think," I say.

I paddle out. The surf is small and disorganized. Dad swims with Adam in the shallows while Mom stands on the beach taking pictures with an Instamatic. On the horizon, a mountainous bank of bluish clouds billows upward sluggishly. Even with everyone nearby it's still slightly spooky being out in the waves alone, as if a clear wall of some sort separates me from them.

When I come in, Mom takes a picture of me and Dad, the board standing upright between us. He combs his hair first. I glance over, reassembling him—the scar on his knee, the shape of his hands and arms, the shoulders I clung to as he glided along the bottoms of swimming pools.

It's hard to believe he's really here, on the beach in Florida, wearing his glasses that have tinted plastic lenses you clip on. Here so briefly, he's like a ghost: here and not here.

Later in the day, we go for a walk in the woods. I show him and Adam the bulldozed clearing, the animal tracks in the sand. We trace their outlines, which crumble if touched. By the mangroves we watch a heron stalking in the shallows, then roll over a log the way Dad taught us, using sticks to lever it up in case a snake is coiled beneath.

A lizard darts across the path and Adam crashes into the underbrush after it.

"You must see a lot of snakes here," Dad says.

"No, I haven't seen a single one. It's strange."

How I miss talking this way, as if pointing out stones in a clear stream.

"Well, you always see them when you least expect to."

"Like that time when you were a kid and you had been hunting them all day without seeing any and then you were eating at a picnic table and one was underneath the table?"

"Right," he says, pleased I've remembered. "Like that."

But it's more than a way of talking that I miss: it's my father.

The next day, in Indialantic, he buys Hang Ten shirts for us at Darcy's. We watch the surfing at the boardwalk, and I tell him the story of the stitches, pointing to the spot in the water where it happened, where I walked up dripping blood.

"My God!" he remarks. "It sounds like you need to be more careful."

"That was months ago. I'm a lot better now."

Adam pulls on his arm. "Have you seen another Zoom Mobile anywhere?"

I roll my eyes. The Zoom Mobile was a toy car with pedals that wound some sort of spring that then propelled it along as if it were running on gas. It disappeared from our driveway in Virginia, and finding another has been one of Adam's obsessions.

Dad drives us to a toy store in Melbourne. As we follow Adam down the air-conditioned aisles, he asks how I like living with Pat.

Here's my chance to overturn the game board and ask to live with him in D.C., though I sense that what he wants to hear is that everything's fine. Which in a way it is. And when it's not, I don't have a choice in the matter. In any case, it's somehow no longer his business.

"I don't know," I say finally. "I love the beach."

"And how's Adam doing?"

Adam calls, "I *hate* Pat!"

———

Dad drives his rental car to the house to say good-bye. He has a tan now. I'm sad, but relieved too: real life can resume.

Adam, as always, is less equivocal. Sobbing, he throws himself into Dad's hip. "Don't go, Dad! *Please* don't go! I don't *want* you to go!"

Dad strokes his hair. "Adam, Adam."

"I *hate* him!"

"Now, Adam."

"I'm coming with you!"

As if in search of inspiration, Dad closes his eyes. "Hey," he says, "why don't you come for a visit at Christmas?"

"I wanna come *now*!"

Mom and I have to pry his arms loose and hold him back from climbing in the car. Dad smiles sadly, waves and drives off.

Adam jerks free. His face is crimson and contorted, snot streaming from his nose.

"I hate all of you!" he bellows.

He runs inside, slamming the front door, then the door to his room. Mom follows.

I watch the rental car go up Surf Road. Turning the corner onto A1A, it's like a body dropping below the surface of the water, stretching out and distorted in the refractions of light.

As I knew I would be, I'm on the verge of tears, uselessly so, then angry for being made to feel that way. Ten minutes later,

Mom drives off in the car and, walking into the woods to get away from them all, I wonder briefly whether she's changed her mind about everything and has gone to stop Dad from taking his plane back to D.C., to ask him to marry her again.

She returns with shopping bags. She's bought a fancy electronic toy for Adam—blatant bribery, though we both know it will work.

"And," she says, "I stopped off at Ron Jon's."

She opens the trunk. There's a beautiful new skateboard inside, made of different-colored strips of wood laminated together.

I ride it up and down the driveway, then coax Adam out of his room and show him how, holding him under the armpits to keep him from falling.

————

Another NASA namesake, the local elementary school is ten miles to the north, in Melbourne Beach proper, a new brick building already cracking in the sun, on the edge of a weedy field.

I sit next to Toby Jackson on the bus. He lives nearby. We've surfed together in the deserted waves of the local beaches, and once at the famous Sebastian Inlet, where I caught a wave that launched me into a sunlit cloud of spray and I floated there for a small eternity, like weather.

As the bus approaches the last stop, we watch out the window for Matt Thyme, who began school two weeks late. With his fine shoulder-length blond hair, chiseled features and sculpted muscles, he resembles a prepubescent Roger Daltry, an idealized cartoon of a surfer boy one of us might draw but who could never really exist.

Yet there he is now in the warm morning light, jeans slung low, T-shirt tossed over one bronzed shoulder. He waits for the bus next to Shark Pit, a spot second in prestige only to Sebastian Inlet: it's but another expression of his royalty.

Matt's father is the shaper Ron Thyme, of Thyme & Crase Surfboards, the line favored by serious older sorts with full beards and stories about trips to Barbados. Each spring, he takes Matt out of school and they sail to Eleuthera, a rib of the Bahamas. What will Matt be doing in Eleuthera when Toby and I are debating whether it's snot or a piece of lint that our teacher, Mr. Pram, is rolling between thumb and index finger? Well, that depends on what time of day it is. In the morning, he eats a mango and paddles over to a reef break with his dad, where they share the fast blue tubes. Around noon, he dons snorkeling gear and spears lobster for lunch. Later, on the deck of the sailboat or, if they feel like it, at a café onshore, he is homeschooled by his (doubtless gorgeous) stepmother, Shelly.

Oh, he's conceited all right. And he alludes to Eleuthera and its point-by-point superiority to Florida with such tiresome frequency that it's become a running joke between Toby and me. But both of us badly want to be his best friend.

"Aloothra!" Toby whispers over his shoulder in imitation of Matt's fluty hippie pronunciation, top lip curled forward as if to blow on a bottle. I giggle conspiratorially.

Matt waits until he's at the top of the steps to slip on his T-shirt, rolling his eyes at the mannish lady bus driver who enforces these bourgeois rules—*shirts worn on the bus.*

Faded and webbed with tiny holes under the arms, it bears a silk-screened Thyme & Crase logo—the yin-yang symbol with Thyme in one half, Crase in the other. Suddenly my yellow Hang Ten shirt seems irredeemably squeaky-clean.

"What's happenin', dudes?"

"Not much!" Toby and I pipe in unison.

Matt flops himself down in the seat across from me (me!), back to the wall of the bus, legs up on the vinyl and crossed at the ankles. He wears some obscure brand of deck shoe.

"Yeah, well, this," Matt waves his arm around at the bus, at school in general, "is definitely not happenin'."

"Did you check it?" I ask him.

"Yep," he says, wobbling one hand to mean: only so-so.

"Aw, man!" He's remembered a wave from the previous day and proceeds to tell us about it. The description is almost purely gestural: hands raised near his eyes, sighting down the fingers, a matter of body language, torque, air pushed through his teeth, as though words lacked both the force and nuance to do justice to the aquadynamic delicacies under consideration.

"That's hot," I say. "I've never surfed Shark Pit."

"Yeah, me neither," Toby adds.

"Well, dude," Matt tells me (me!), "you should come over after school sometime. I'll lend you a board."

"Definitely!" I tell him. "Definitely!"

The following week, I bring my baggies to school rolled up in a towel. The waves have been good for the past two days and the cars parked at Shark Pit mean they're probably good again today.

Matt and I scamper off the bus, cross A1A and see in a glimpse that the waves are three to four feet, the swells approaching shore in well-defined lines from far out. We pivot as if rounding a base and run back across A1A and up a dirt road toward Matt's house.

"It's like corduroy, dude!" he exclaims over his shoulder. Could he have just coined that wonderful phrase?

He takes a path paved with flagstones and I follow, tagging the ragged leaves of the banana trees lining it.

"That's where my dad and Shelly live," he says as we pass a house. "I live back here."

He has his own little cottage! It's too much: the perfection of his life is crushing.

Inside there's a coffee table covered with seashells, copies of *Surfer* strewn on the bed, a desk with a reading lamp. It smells of incense, surf wax and pot.

We tear off our clothes and clamber into baggies.

Leaning against one wall are three boards, all bearing the Thyme & Crase logo like a family crest. Matt looks me up and down then flutters his fingers before them as if choosing chocolates. "For you, dude, this one, definitely."

He passes me a thin yellow board shaped like a teardrop. "You're sort of a power type, I can tell."

I smile, deeply pleased, and heft it—it's so light mine seems like solid wood by comparison.

Matt tucks another board under his arm and trots out the door. "Let's tell Dad about the waves first."

"Dad"—as though he's my father too.

Ron Thyme sits shirtless at a table, foam dust in the hairs of his forearms, the muscles of his torso a Roman breastplate. He's peeling the thick rind from a navel orange.

He grins broadly at us. "I guess I don't need to ask how the waves are!" He looks like Thor in my *Norse Gods and Goddesses* book: bright blue eyes, a handlebar mustache, a corona of curly hair encircling his fine-featured face.

"They're pretty hot, Dad!"

Next to the bowl of fruit, as if simply another part of a wholesome snack, is a plastic sack of pot.

A beautiful woman has looked up from a shirt she's embroidering on the couch. This must be Shelly.

Now what has to happen in order for me to be adopted by this family, absorbed into its higher order?

Shelly says, "What's the homework situation, Matt?"

"Not too bad."

"You'll show me later, okay?"

"You got it."

As we make our way out into the dark blue water, I stay as close to Matt as I'm able, and not simply to suggest that we're equals. It's dangerous out here. Colorful boards flash past, back and arm muscles flexing as men fly through the air over the tops of waves, the spray of which loops backward in a hard offshore wind. Like long twisting sentences, the waves are hard for me to read, though Matt seems to know them by heart.

We lose track of each other; then, toward sundown, I hear a high voice shout, "Hey!"

There he is, a little farther out than the pack and paddling for what is surely the "wave of the day," the biggest and best to come through. The ruffled stretch of water in front has been drawn tight, like the apron of a stage, and Matt is lit by a band of sunlight at its peak.

But two bearded giants are also paddling for it and my heart beats faster, out of both envy and fear.

"Hey!" he barks again. "My wave!"

"We'll see about that," I think.

"I *got* it!"

How he manages to shout and paddle at the same time is beyond me, but what's truly amazing is that he has the guts to shout at grown men in the first place.

Suddenly he's on his feet in a low crouch, arms spread from the steep drop, long hair blown back like that of an Indian leaping from a cliff. It's a picture straight out of *Surfer*.

The men see it too, and, with a show of begrudging respect, both cease paddling and sit up on their boards. Rapt, the crowd watches Matt and wave as they roll by, heads moving together as though following the flight of a meteor.

"*All right, Matt!*" I call, meaning also: "*That's my friend!*"

Well, I thought he would be good, but not this good. I make a quick calculation: Matt's been surfing since he was eight. That's two years or so. I've been surfing for eight months. That's not even a year.

When I've been surfing for two years, will I be as good as Matt is, or will he always be this much better than I am? And how, if I can't catch up, can I be his best friend?

———

In childhood, when the heart is open, a best friend means so much. Mine appears in unexpected form. His name is Carson Reynolds, and almost immediately we take to looking back fondly on our first encounter: at the end of a school day my bus is about to pull out and Carson, student patrol sash and badge over a snow-white Hang Ten shirt, blocks my way at a crosswalk.

"Wait!" he says, bumping me with his forearms. "Until I say you can go!"

He's big, but I'm as big or bigger than anyone now, and, accustomed to the privileges of size, I shove him aside and saunter to my bus. Secretly, Carson admires this disdain and not long afterward, as a tender of friendship, he quits the student patrol.

In the evenings we speak on the phone. If there have been waves, Carson does most of the talking, since I've usually gone out alone and find it hard to articulate much about the experience, which is enchanted but distorted by solitude, a dream watched over at best by a lone fisherman. In Melbourne Beach, Carson surfs along the edges of an extended clique of older surfers, a kind of floating clan, full of social nuance, jealousies, microallegiances. I can't keep all the names straight but Carson recounts the highlights as though I can.

"Then this peak came to me and Billy, okay? And I was right there but he didn't see me and neither did Ethan—"

"Ethan?"

"Larry's little brother."

"Oh, yeah," I say, feigning to remember so as to avoid another genealogy.

"Anyway, then they both saw me and Billy pulled up and said, 'Go!'"

"Wow."

"I couldn't believe it!"

"Then what happened?"

"I got totally tubed!"

I sigh. When will I be part of life again, witnessed by others? There's hope: Mom and Pat have been driving into Melbourne

Beach to look at houses. Pat says he's tired of the long drive to town and to his job in Melbourne, but the secret reason is that Mom's pregnant and we'll need more room, though it's possible I'm imagining this.

Meanwhile, Carson invites me to spend the night and, hoping to make an impression on him and his heroes, I persuade Mom to drop me off at school on Friday with my board. This way, instead of having to borrow a strange one or wait for her to drive into town Saturday, I can have it with me early the next morning.

I don't know for certain that it's against the rules to bring a surfboard to school, but I imagine it is and have devised a hazy plot of stashing the board somewhere on the grounds before any adults notice it.

Students waiting in amoebic groups near the front office spot the board; a few point and shout things I can't make out.

Idling the car, Mom says, "Are you sure this is all right?"

"Yes! I got special permission!"

Looking around, I slide the board out through the sunroof and stand it in the lawn by the flagpole, then wave as casually as I'm able while she drives off.

I head for a hedge alongside the far side of the building but before I can reach it, Matt, Carson and Toby break away from the crowd and converge on the board.

Carson smiles and shakes his head. "I can't believe you really brought it to school!"

Matt is unfazed. "May I?" He slips it from under my arm, stands it in the grass and sights leisurely along the rail. "Not much rocker, dude."

"It rides okay," I reply distractedly.

Toby looks up. "Uh-oh."

The assistant principal, a stocky man who does the school's disciplinary work, is marching across the grass, thick forearm shielding his eyes against the sunlight.

"Whose is that?" he calls, dodging a sprinkler.

"Mine," I tell him.

"It's mine now."

Matt says, "Don't you have your own board, dude?"

Upon us, the assistant principal focuses his small eyes on Matt. "Smart off again."

"I was just askin'."

"Smart off one more time."

The assistant principal seizes the board by the rails and pries it from Matt's hands.

"When can I get it back?" I ask.

"We'll see," he says over his shoulder.

"Wha—?"

"I said, we'll see."

"You can't do that!" calls Carson. "You can't just keep his board!"

"Watch me, mister!"

"Look how he carries it, the kook!" Matt stage-whispers behind a hand.

Toby says, "'Smart off one more time!'"

"Don't worry, Thad!" Carson shouts. "My mom'll get it back, no problem!"

Carson's mother won't allow him to be paddled. "They can't touch me!" he's fond of saying. "And they know it!"

Matt scoffs, "What's he think you're going to do with it? Like you can surf in the fuckin' hallway!"

We do surf in the hallway: pretend the walls are waves and drag our fingers across the bricks, hoot as we emerge into the light of a classroom. Nothing matches the delights of surfing, so its stylings crop up within and overtake everything: banking on our bikes, pivoting around the bases in kickball, doodling, even guiding streams of piss through S-turns.

But with my board in custody, I'm glum and can only wait anxiously for the end of the day.

At last it's three o'clock. Carson and I meet by the flagpole to wait for his mother. He scans the sky. He's on a swim team at the Eau Gallie Yacht Club and his blond bangs are slightly green from chlorine. A cover of pinkish clouds is moving across the pale blue of the sky from the south.

"This looks like a front."

"Is that good?"

"Oh, yeah," he says. "We'll have waves tomorrow."

We hear a car beep twice and turn to see Mrs. Reynolds pulling up in a red sports-car convertible, top down.

"All right!" Carson says. "The Fiat!"

"Hi, guys!"

"Hi, Mom!"

Glamorous, she has a dark tan, a brown flip hairdo, large sunglasses. "Where's Thad's board?" Carson confided my plan to her the night before.

She listens with growing irritation as he explains what happened, then turns off the ignition and walks to the front office. Carson and I follow.

"May I help you?" asks one of the secretaries, but Mrs. Reynolds sweeps past them. We hear a duet of voices—hers and the assistant principal's—then she emerges from his office with the board and waves me over to take it, still talking. "Well, he won't do it again, but for God's sake, it's just a surfboard!"

"Check to see if he dinged it!" Carson calls but I ignore him and carry the board to the car before the assistant principal changes his mind.

We slide it nose-down into a space behind the seats and squeeze into the front, Carson sitting on my lap.

"Thanks, Mrs. Reynolds!" I say.

"You're welcome, honey."

Satisfied, Carson says, "See? No problem."

As we drive away from the school, he says, "Do it, Mom, do it!"

Tooting the horn, Mrs. Reynolds downshifts—her right wrist has a pale circle from a sweatband—and guides the car up onto the bike path, kids squealing deliriously as she weaves slowly through them.

Carson giggles and honks the horn, but when he grabs the wheel she swats his hand away.

We stop to check the surf at a small boardwalk in Melbourne Beach. The waves are small and blown out.

"Don't worry," Carson says, "it's supposed to get better tomorrow."

Backing the car out, Mrs. Reynolds says, "Someone still has chores to do."

"I already did 'em!"

"Don't shout, son. The Colonel said something about bar glasses." Carson crosses his arms and pouts, his weight crushing my lap.

"The Colonel?" I whisper.

"My *stepdad*."

Built on a corner a block or so from the beach, their house is large, two stories, with a screened-in pool in back. Mrs. Reynolds pulls up beside a brown Cadillac in the driveway but keeps the car running.

"I'm going to the base for groceries."

Carson and I slide the board out of the back. "Now, if I were you, I'd take care of those bar glasses."

He ignores her.

"Carson."

"Okay!" He slams the car door.

"You're cruisin', mister!" she says over the whine of the reversing car.

Frowning, Carson carries my board into the pantry and leans it next to his, the rail of which he caresses, face clearing. "Check it out! David Nuuwiha custom-shaped it for me in Huntington Beach, where my real dad lives." David Nuuwiha is a surf star with a rock star's penchant for fur coats and Bentleys.

"Carson!"

We jump. A man looms in the doorway to the kitchen. He's tall and slightly stooped, with narrow steely eyes. The left one twitches three or four times then stops.

"Sir?"

"Prints all over this highball glass." He has a southern accent.

Carson tilts his head to one side as if not quite understanding, his voice rising an octave. "Sir?"

The Colonel presses his lips together. "Prints all over this *highball glass*." He waggles the tumbler with sinister festiveness.

"But I—"

The Colonel silences him with a grim smile, crooks a finger and retreats.

Carson's head falls forward. "I'll be back in a minute," he mumbles.

The bottom of Carson's board is misted with airbrush designs—dolphins, suns, stars—in a tasteful prism of apricot, raspberry, lemon, cerulean. It's like some unspeakably luxurious sedan.

I go into the kitchen and stare out through the sliding-glass door at the motionless pool, the screen porch, the backyard. Through another sliding-glass door across the patio, I see Carson standing before the Colonel, who sits on a couch, gesturing with a pair of tongs.

Carson shuffles out and the Colonel, using tongs, drops an ice cube into a glass. Carson pokes his head around a corner and I follow him up the polished wooden stairs and into his room.

When I close the door, he throws himself facedown on his bed and shouts into a pillow, "I'm grounded!"

"For what?"

"You're supposed to hold a highball glass like this"—he holds up one hand—"with your fingers inside the glass so you won't get fingerprints on it, see?"

I don't, but shrug. "The surf sucks anyway."

"But I wanted to take you to the Youth Center!"

"Maybe your mom will do something," I offer hopefully, but he only groans.

"What's wrong with his eye?"

"He was in Vietnam!" Carson says in a sarcastic woe-is-me tone.

"Oh."

"Boo-hoo! He flew fighter jets. Boo-hoo!"

I notice a poster above the bed. "Who's that?"

"Who?"

"In the poster." It looks like a pouty Jesus in leather pants. He follows my gaze. "Jim Morrison."

I point to another one, of a homely woman wearing a feather boa. "And that?"

Now he sits up. "Janis Joplin. I love her."

"You have the coolest room." I say this to cheer him up but it's also true.

"My stepsister Karen gave them to me when she went to college." Coming out of his funk, he points to crates stuffed with albums lining one wall. "Along with her record collection."

"Wow."

"Here, this is Janis." He turns on the stereo and puts the needle down on a record. On the treasure-chest trunk beside the stereo, there's a sculpture of a wrinkled tube of Crest. But instead of toothpaste, what's squeezed out is a coil of gunk— sawdust, tacks, bits of metal.

"Karen did that in art class. She's kind of a genius."

"For sure. What's it made of?"

"Papier-mâché, mostly."

"I can't believe how much it looks like a real tube of Crest."

"She's super talented."

I sit on the bed and touch the sculpture. It's the greatest work of art I've ever seen.

At dinner, almost nothing is said. There's the scrape of silverware, the subdued noises of food being chewed in a disciplined fashion. Carson's older sister, Marshall, thirteen, takes my measure.

"May Thad and I be excused from the table?" Carson asks.

Mrs. Reynolds turns to the Colonel. "Perry?"

He finishes chewing a morsel of roast beef, sips red wine, blots his lips with a cloth napkin and nods.

Back up in Carson's room, while looking through his collection of *Surfer* magazines, we listen to Led Zeppelin, Janis Joplin, Jim Morrison, the Who.

We study an airbrushed ad for the upcoming surf film *Pacific Vibrations,* which Carson has torn out of an issue of *Surfer* and taped to the wall over his bed: a cartoon sun with slot eyes and gasping mouth bursts from the sea, molten blobs of heat and water spraying in a fan above it, while in the middle ground a perfect wave breaks in both directions, squirting tendrils of Lava-lamp-like spray from its tube.

We take turns lying down on his bed, paddling, hopping to our feet, making the roar of the waves, the spray in the offshore wind, the howls of other surfers, the commentary of experts. As the waves get bigger, we turn the music up.

"This!" Carson shouts over Hendrix, "is me at Sunset!"

He strokes to the beat of the music on the crocheted comforter, hops to his feet and rides a treacherously steep windblown peak from the outside through to the inside bowl, where he's tubed repeatedly and then kicks out stylishly, a look of supreme nonchalance on his face.

"Here's me," I crow, "at Pipeline!" I stand looking around wide-eyed at the innards of a gigantic deadly tube.

Carson turns up the volume a bit more and paddles out at Waimea.

When the Colonel jerks open the door, Carson's crouched at the top of the biggest wave in the history of the world and of surfing, and I'm bobbing on the carpet filming him with a water-proof movie camera.

The Colonel leans past the threshold for a better look at this scene, long fingers gripping the door frame. His eye twitches.

Catching sight of him, Carson freezes then leaps to turn off the music.

The Colonel remains silent, then says simply, "Keep it down."

"Yes, sir."

"Do you read me?"

"Yes, sir."

He closes the door softly. Carson remains watchful. I see why: a few seconds later the door opens again and the Colonel crooks a finger at Carson, who goes out with head hung low.

I hear their voices then the door opens, Carson comes in, closes it and hurls himself onto the bed, where he sobs loudly into his pillow then comes up laughing.

"Fooled you!"

For this I wrestle him to the floor and pin him. "Say 'Uncle'!"

"Get off me!"

"Say it!"

"Get off!"

He writhes from side to side, cheek crushed in the Persian rug, until he's on the verge of truly crying and I begin to worry that when I do let him up he'll throw something at me or otherwise go berserk.

"Promise not to flip out?"

"Get *off*!"

I stand and back away as if terrified. Carson laughs and the air clears.

We fall asleep in our baggies, whispering about waves and

surf stars Barry Kanaiapuni, Nat Young, Jock Sutherland and David Nuuwiha (whose stance, I think, is too wide, while Carson adores his style, so I keep quiet on this point), how good the surf might be in the morning, how good it might be later in the fall, school and the blond girl named Lisa we both love, surfing before school, the way sharks are said to feed at dawn.

We're up by seven. Clenching our morning erections, we creep downstairs, grab the boards from the pantry and pee in a hedge.

Chanting, "Oh please let there be waves!" we jog to the beach, taking a path between two houses, beneath young pine trees bowing toward each other to form a kind of colonnade, at the end of which we see a three-foot wave breaking hard.

"I told you!" Carson crows.

We hoot, grin and punch each other in the arm, hopping up and down in the sand like gold miners at an open vein of ore.

A warm rain begins to fall and we dash into the water. Having been humbled by Matt Thyme, I'm relieved to see that Carson surfs slightly less well than I do: though he falls with great flair, he still falls. He seems to enjoy the drama of it.

"You—" Carson says as I paddle up beside him.

"Yeah?"

"You're a switch-foot!" He means I can put either foot forward and so always surf facing the wave. It's a kind of ambidexterity.

"I guess so."

"But that's bitchin'!"

I shrug.

"You know, though," he says, "backside is cool too. You should try it."

A good peak lurches up in front of Carson. "Let me have this wave and I will!"

"Deal!"

In this way, I begin losing the feel for surfing switch-foot, the value of which we fail to grasp, though eventually it becomes another of our stories: how Carson persuaded me that it was "cool" to surf backside.

After a while, in threes and fours, the clique of older surfers, twenty or so in all, paddles out to the north of us. They begin noisily enjoying themselves. Carson waves for me to follow and we make our way over to their perimeter.

"That's Billy," Carson whispers, pointing discreetly, as at celebrities. "That's Muhler, and the one talking to him is Ethan." They look to be about seventeen.

After a bit, Billy glances over at us and Carson waves, pipes, "Hey, Billy!"

The distracted way the older surfer nods back leads me to conclude that Carson is less familiar to them than they are to him. But this only means they're authentic, worth pursuing. What are we, after all?

When one of the clique gets a good wave, the others who see it shout "All right, now!" like the amen corner in a Baptist church. I practice it under my breath: "All right, now!"

The weather lowers, the rain falls harder. There's a whiff of wood smoke in the air from the chimneys of the beach houses. It mixes with the clouds scraping through the tall Australian pines that line the shore, their branches embowering the roofs of the houses. All this, combined with the English-ballad-influenced Led Zeppelin in my head, creates an enchanted, medieval atmosphere.

To the north, upward and slightly obscured by curtains of rain, are the golden-haired knights whose recognition I've silently vowed to win, while beside me, the rail of his board bumping mine as we pass over a wave, is my new best friend and fellow squire.

We grin maniacally at each other, awareness of surfing's magic flowing back and forth between us like a current. I feel that magic deepening, being given to me again, a new body I slip into, and am suddenly so happy I burst into tears, plunging my head underwater so Carson won't see.

When Mom picks me up, I sense something has happened, something for the better.

"So you like Melbourne Beach?"

"I love it!"

"Do you want to see our new house?"

It's just a few blocks from Carson's, the streets between named after the trees and flowers you see everywhere: hibiscus, banyan, jasmine, mango. The house is on a corner, long, one story, with white stucco walls and white shingles.

We walk around. The lawn is large and green, with a banjo fig near the driveway.

There are graced surf towns—Santa Cruz, Bolinas, Malibu, Montauk—where cars rust like lace, people ride bikes in the soft dusk, wave with brown hands, call to each other by name. The coastline is seen from atop swells through powdery light, wet suits gleam like seals. Shielded for a certain period, suffused with beauty and with subtler blessings, innocence, a certain sweetness, they are as worlds out of time, these towns.

Melbourne Beach was such a place.

Five

The Christmas tree is hung with strands of tinsel, sprayed with aerosol snow, references to northern winters nearly lost in translation here.

"Oh my God!"

Adam is holding the yellow board at arm's length, as if to get a better look at a relative long lost and presumed dead.

It's a used knee board, shaped like a squat spoon. I picked it out. It's his height and thick enough for him to ride standing up. On the bottom is a pen-and-ink drawing of a pig wearing jeans, a hat and striped shirt, and beneath it "Arnold Zieffel."

Above all, it's permission to enter the world offshore—the real one, that is. He's eight.

Mom gazes gravely into my eyes. "You look out for him now."

"I will," I tell her, "don't worry."

I received a wet suit, an O'Neill long john. I'm stretching one of the legs on over a foot.

Pat has opened one of his presents. "Hey, hey, hey!" he says.

It's a device that heats up shaving cream. He seems genuinely delighted. May I never grow up.

"No stitches," she continues.

"No way." I hope not, anyway. I think back to the gloom and fear of my first days. I can spare Adam the solitude and ignorance, at least.

My stocking is stuffed with bars of Sex Wax, a T-shirt from Darcy's Surf Shop, notice of a renewed subscription to *Surfer*.

Is there a greater mother in the world?

———

The waves are glassy as ice sculptures, the sky Arctic blue, so high and stretched so thin that it seems on the verge of vanishing, of revealing all.

"Hey," I say, indicating a wave with my chin. Adam's teeth are chattering. We're wearing wet suits.

He nods and paddles for it with dainty, cat-paw strokes. I watch hopefully. It's his third morning out and he's yet to stand up.

He rides it on his belly again. This is getting embarrassing.

I scan the beach—still deserted, but it won't be for much longer.

"That was good," I say when he's made his way back out. "You've got the swing of *catching* waves, anyway."

"It's easy!"

I take a breath. "Try standing up—that's not so easy."

"That one was too small to ride standing up," he informs me.

"Wait for a bigger one, then."

He nods and sits up to watch the horizon, hands placed carefully on the rails. When they see him with the board, people smile: the outline echoes the shape of his round head and pageboy haircut. I worry that his concentration and seriousness are being corrupted by all this attention to cuteness.

"Okay, now," I say, "here comes one."

His eyes widen.

"Circle your feet like I told you." He churns his legs and the nose of the board swings around toward shore. "Wait—what do you think? Is it going to break?"

"No," he decides. He looks relieved.

"Right," I say as the wave lifts us together. "Good."

Behind it is a bigger one.

"Okay," I say, "how about this one?"

"Yeah, it's gonna break." He pauses. "Right?"

"Right, so *paddle*."

I turn toward the beach as I say this. There I see Billy Olin, Brandon and Ethan, boards under arms. They've just begun to acknowledge my existence and I'm tempted to take the wave myself, if only to prevent Adam from soiling the family name with an ignominious belly ride.

Instead, I shove the tail of his board to be sure he doesn't miss. It's as if I've christened a ship: he climbs to his feet by way of one knee, as though genuflecting, then swings off down the wave and out of view.

Hallelujah!

I hoot and so do Billy and the others on the beach.

Twenty yards farther along, the board pinwheels through the air and washes in.

I watch the backside of the wave, the cape of marbled foam. He should have come up by now. Oh, God!

I sprint paddle for the spot where the board shot loose. Then Adam's round head bobs up like a cantaloupe. I hear him cough once. He turns and swims for shore.

Eventually, dour Brandon paddles up, deltoids rippling intricately, like plumage in a breeze.

I keep my eyes averted from his hands. The middle and ring fingers of one were blown off by an M-80, a Fourth of July accident. Bristles sprout from the stumps. I attribute his glumness to the mangled hand, but it could also be his father, a doctor, and the pressure he keeps Brandon under to get into medical school. That alone would sour me on life.

He looks back toward shore, where Adam is running up the sand to retrieve Arnold. My little brother—I must watch out for him, must never let anything bad happen.

"Was that his first wave?"

"Yep!"

Brandon shakes his head, droplets sprinkling the surface musically.

"Another lost generation." It's hard to tell how serious he is—or what he means, for that matter.

I laugh uncertainly. "For sure!"

"For sure," he echoes, paddling away.

"Did you see that?" Adam shouts as he clears the top of a wave. "I stood up!"

He's wearing the crazed, slightly daft expression of the convert.

"I saw you."

"I can surf now!"

I raise my brows skeptically, hoping the others are out of earshot.

"*I can.*"

And it's essentially true. He stands up again and again, always with the slight hitch, as if he's curtsying to the wave. On his face, a beseeching expression.

Toward noon, whitecaps appear on the horizon and the surf turns choppy. Adam rides his bike ahead of me, swooping into triumphant S-turns, obviously aching to tell Mom the news.

In the backyard, Pat is taking pictures of her, the wind that ruined the waves blowing through her new Shirley Partridge shag. She's turned sideways to show the great curve of her belly, the sight of which gives me a mild jolt. I've forgotten about it.

"Mom!" Adam calls. We coast to a halt by the spigot, where we rinse the sand from our feet and drop our bikes in the grass.

"Mom, I did it! I stood up! I can surf!"

"That's great, honey!"

Is her being pregnant good news or bad? What I want is not to have to think about it at all, for it not to matter. But it matters, all right.

Pat cranks the rewind. "One more, little mama."

Can't he wait until the baby's born before starting in with the "mama" stuff? Well, he's happier, at least.

Adam rinses the sand off his ankles then begins moving the stream of water carefully over the surface of his board.

I snatch the hose. "It's not gonna rust!"

"Hey!" he calls. "Take one of me and Arnold!"

Pat looks over at us.

"All right," he says. "Come on, Arnold!"

Because swells seldom last more than two or three days, when one arrives, everyone surfs until faint with hunger and exhaustion. Among the last to leave, Adam and I trudge up the beach. We've waited too long. We're in a kind of despair, almost a fugue state. Our swollen mouths drool strings of seawater on the sand; the boards seem odd and out of place under our arms, like objects salvaged at random from a burning house.

At home, the new Volvo station wagon is missing from the garage and inside, the house is quiet. We bump into furniture in the dimness.

With trembling hands, I cook bacon and eggs. Adam toasts and butters a stack of whole-wheat bread. We've done this before, have established a division of labor. Neither of us speaks, though Adam's begun whining from hunger.

"Cut it out!"

Finally we lay the bacon on the toast and the eggs on the bacon and, standing at the stove, raise this greatest of dishes to our cracked lips. Hot yolk squirts, trickles down our chins.

My eyes are squeezed shut. "God!"

"Man!" says Adam. We're like the survivors of some cataclysm restating first principles.

We adjourn to the kitchen table and slather toast with health-food peanut butter, drizzling it with honey. Adam sprinkles his with wheat germ. We drink tall glasses of milk. We're blinking our eyes, coming back to life.

The station wagon rumbles into the garage and falls silent. I pause mid-chew and survey the eggshells, dirty pan, the stack of toast. In the wrong mood, Pat sees these après-surf meals as show-offish gluttony, but there's no time to clean up. And it might be Mom.

It's Pat. He nods at us distractedly and lights a Tareyton at the sink.

"Where's Mom?" I ask him.

"The baby came last night!" he announces, smiling strangely.

"The baby?" Adam cries, dropping his knife.

"Yep," Pat says. He's taken a bottle of vodka down from the cabinet above the sink. "You guys have a little brother! How about that?"

"Wow!" I say, peering at him. He rarely drinks.

Adam claps like a seal. "Wow, wow, *wow*!"

Something is wrong. Pat's face looks gray, the cigarette trembles.

"So is Mom okay?" He's adding orange juice to three fingers of vodka he's poured into a glass. He takes a gulp.

"Yeah," he says, "she's fine." He pauses. "But the baby came a little early."

"Early?"

"He's premature. Tiny. They have him in an incubator."

"Is he going to be okay?"

"Sure," Pat says. He doesn't seem sure. He seems shaken, afraid. If I ever wished for this, I know better now. It's like the shadowy form of a predator floating into view.

"He'll be okay." Suddenly I feel protective of him, of us all.

He tosses back the drink, then brings the glass down with a clank. "I hope you're right."

"He will," I insist. I don't know what else to say. "He will."

Two days later, I'm rinsing off with the hose in the yard. On the patio there is now a rack for our boards. Pat built it out of plywood and painted it green. I slide the twin fin into it and go inside.

Mom emerges from the hallway with outstretched arms, like a monster. It startles me. She's back from the hospital.

"I need a hug!"

I give her one, reluctantly. Her drawn face and her neediness repel me. Having a baby was her idea, not mine.

Under the blue muumuu, her breasts are bigger. Would she have had them enlarged while she was in the hospital?

"Come see the baby."

I follow her to the room across from mine, where a crib has been set up. I stand beside her, rest my hands on the wooden railing.

She draws aside a diaphanous white blanket. He's tiny and red, rubbery, curled like a crustacean, a hermit crab perished between shells. The matted hair is dark, like Pat's. He seems of a different race, a different species, even.

"We're going to call him Jason."

"Huh."

What I want to know is whether he's going to grow into Pat's little taskmaster, his informant.

"Daddy!" I hear him calling. "The lawn's not mowed properly! He's Polish!"

"Daddy, there's still crumbs on the counter where he wiped with the sponge!"

Sluggish with the sweet fatigue of having surfed most of another day, I carry my board up the beach through long, late-afternoon shadows. It's summer again, my second in Florida, but have I ever lived elsewhere, ever not surfed? Worn Bermuda shorts instead of baggies, penny loafers rather than sneakers or flip-flops? That was someone else, that chubby, pale boy—a larval stage.

I prod my stomach—it burns from wax rash—and pause to look back at the surf.

It's still good—a quick hollow peak, middle-break—though only one kid, unfamiliar to me, is still out, paddling with the coltish eagerness of a beginner. He looks tiny and stick-like in the vast chalky blue of sky and ocean. Sidestepping a Portuguese man-of-war, I wait with a certain noblesse oblige to see if he'll manage to catch a wave.

My own surfing has recently won the cautious, connoisseur-like approval of Billy and company, and I feel entitled to condescend. It was Carson who introduced me to them, but since he's often at tennis practice, I've had to make my own way—the culmination of which was being invited to Ben's house for a screening of their latest home surf movie.

It was projected onto the bedroom wall. Ben's father is missing in action; the son's silver memorial bracelet gleamed in the light leaking from the grille of the projector.

The kid paddles for a wave but fails to catch it and I turn away. The shadows fallen across the sand are cast by a stand of enormous Australian pines, which rise up in the vacant lot we use to reach the beach. It's called Billy's, this spot, since it's the beach closest to Billy Olin's and where he surfs most often.

Quick-witted, with a head of tight Adonis-like blond curls and a compact muscular body, Billy is the most golden of the Golden Boys. I have to ride out of my way to get here, but I do so gladly, because being in Billy's presence is like appearing in a movie with Paul Newman, like *Butch Cassidy and the Sundance Kid,* where everything turns out all right and he winks at you in the end.

I walk like Billy (with a strut), and I talk like Billy (nasal, ironic). I even imitate his tic of puckering his lips when he's concentrating hard. I wear the same brand of sheer baggies that Billy wears, despite the fact that they get so transparent when wet that girls can see everything unless you arrange yourself carefully beneath the velcro fly. And of course I try to surf like Billy.

I got to see how much when suddenly I was paddling for a wave in the film. It was as if a surprise birthday cake crowded with lit candles were being borne into the room. I watched as I hopped to my feet, did a Billy-like sideslip and was briefly enveloped by a caul of clear water, blushing at the hoots.

———

At the crest of the beach, I step over what remains of a low fence built by a realty company. The top board has been kicked away, the shattered remnants of it scattered through a bed of sea grapes.

The shadow is thick and my tanned skin appears darker here, the palms of my hands glowing white in contrast to the nut-brown of the rest.

By the trunk of an Australian pine is a circle of about fifteen people. I can't make out who they are, but as I draw closer I recognize the deep voice of Pete.

He's imitating a southern sheriff: "'Boy, your eyes are as *red as foxfire!*'" It's the end of a story. Everyone is laughing.

Pete confers with someone then calls, "Wanna smoke a dube?"

"Sure," I say, grateful that Adam went home earlier.

I set my twin fin on the ground and sit cross-legged like the others, most of them teenage girls I've seen around but don't know, their heads silhouetted against a smear of orange sunset.

Someone says, "Thad the man." It's Ethan—I can tell by his bush of hair.

The papers glint in Pete's fingers. I relish the secretive, vaguely sexual texture of these preparations—the shapes taken by the pot inside the Baggie, its weight and aroma, the passing of the joints, the way the Baggie is sealed with a lick of the tongue. Whether I like the high itself is less certain.

A week ago I smoked with Chris Bush, a thirteen-year-old I met at the boardwalk. He and his older brother are being groomed for surf stardom by Gary Propper, the most famous surfer on the East Coast, and simply being at Chris's house was thrilling. He called two girls. They were older—thirteen or fourteen—wearing bikinis. We drank cooking sherry, then Chris took the prettier of the two into his room and I went with the other into his parent's room and sat beside her on the edge of the tall, neatly made bed. She looked at me under bright blue eyelids, and I kissed her. She had a chipped front tooth. Then I gently pushed her back on the bed and slid one hand down along her stomach and into her bikini bottom, but she grabbed my wrist when I tried to take it off and I wasn't sure what else to do.

At noon the father, a plumber with Elvis hair and large sad eyes, came home, and the girls scampered down the hall and climbed out a window. Casting suspicious looks at us, he ate lunch in the kitchen then left in his truck. Chris cut a hole in the tube from a roll of toilet paper, covered the hole with tinfoil and punctured the tinfoil with a fork. We sat in the sunlight on the wood floor of the small living room and smoked pot, the seeds exploding when we held a match to the bowl. The sunlight seemed to stay fallen in the same rectangle for hours. That was probably the best time.

But on the horizon of any high, however good, inevitably appears the dark cloud of Pat.

"One second there," he said as I floated past the couch in the living room.

"Don't you say hello anymore?" The *Wide World of Sports* was on TV. My eyes felt like bloodshot eggs served up on my cheeks.

"I said 'Hi.'" Suddenly I wasn't sure I had said it aloud.

"Then I stand corrected. I must not have heard you."

"Sorry," I said.

I slunk down the hall. I had made it past the troll.

Then I heard him call my name. Catching a glimpse of my stunned face in the bathroom mirror, I said a brief prayer and shuffled back into the living room.

"I wasn't finished."

"Oh."

He gestured at the TV. "Your mother and I watched a program about drugs earlier."

I frowned. What an odd subject to bring up.

"I have to tell you, though, I didn't learn anything I didn't already know," he said wearily.

"That's good," I thought, beginning to imagine telling my friends the story. "Because I'm stoned right now."

He tapped his tire-tread sandal. I stared at the large toe of his right foot. Sober and clean, tufted with wiry black hairs and angling away toward the others, it was like a small toe version— a toe portrait!—of the man.

I felt a chuckle rise in my chest and to curtail it, said, "I don't do drugs."

"No, I didn't think so."

He watched the TV, one foot tapping. He drew a breath to say something more, then waved his hand, dismissing me.

———

Having lit another long, lumpy joint, Pete leans back with his elbow held high and, to laughter, takes an enormous toke, puffing out his cheeks like a trumpet player.

It reaches me by way of a girl wearing a red halter top, her fingers brushing against mine, and as I bring the joint to my lips I sense a collective twinkle of admiration in their eyes.

"This kid," someone usually says, "is so much cooler than I was at that age." If only I felt as cool as I looked.

Now an older surfer named Weaver taps my elbow, proffering a joint. When did he get here? Waxy scars flow over the tops of his hands and fingers from under a long-sleeve shirt, which he wears no matter how hot it is, even in the water. The story I've heard is that he was glassing a board while smoking a joint and dropped a lit match into a bucket of resin or acetone and in the explosion caught fire.

There are more stories, a whirl of them, like sparks ascending from a bonfire. Billy himself took mescaline and ran through a sliding-glass door—his forearms are sprayed with scars—and now he doesn't even smoke pot. He says he's "retired."

Cars have their headlights on now, and as they turn onto the highway the beams sweep across us, illuminating faces.

I'm not sure how many joints have gone around—six, seven. I feel as though I'm perched in some kind of buzzing energy field. And my heart: it's beating too hard, too fast.

"I better get going," I announce, my voice distant and reedy. "Thanks." I stand up.

"Okay," says Ethan.

"That's cool," croons the girl beside me, smiling with Madonna-like sadness at the ground.

To the joint in his hand, Pete says, "Yeah, maybe we should, uh, get going too. Huh, Ethan?"

But Ethan says nothing and no one else stirs. Pete blows on the joint to remove a ragged piece of paper.

Where's my board? It's behind me. I pick it up and start toward the road and my bike, walking very slowly over the pine needles, legs cut in half by a car's headlights.

I pause, listen to my heartbeat, walk a bit, then pause again.

"Thad!" Ethan calls.

"Yes?" Something about this makes a few people laugh. The difference between "yes" and "yeah."

"You all right?"

"I *think* so." More laughter.

I laugh too, but when I stop, my heart feels as though it's trying to shoulder its way through the wall of my chest. I walk a few steps, place a hand on my chest, then walk a little farther.

At the fence, I sit on the top rail to listen some more. Now I'm having trouble breathing.

I pick up my bike, which has tipped over, its pedals entangled with two other bikes on the strip of grass. It's brighter here, out from under the trees of the lot, but the sun's nearly gone.

I look down A1A. The approach of cars is a low ominous whine. It thickens into a sort of porridge as they draw near, then shatters around me. Finally I scamper across and jog slowly along beside the bike.

I stop to listen to my heart. It's worse. If I have to tell Mom and Pat, what will happen? Will we go to the emergency room? I'll have to admit that I smoke pot.

Suddenly it occurs to me that Pat *knew I was high that day.* I stop walking.

Of course he knew! He was telling me so, only indirectly. How can I go home now? But I have to: I might be having a heart attack!

I take a few steps, pause. The house next to the road has its lights on. I'm staring at the wooden gate of the fence, which is slightly ajar, as if it's about to open farther.

Someone's coming up the street. It's Pat, with a surfboard. He was planning to paddle it out and capture me.

I stop and close my eyes, braced for a blow. When it doesn't come, I open them.

It's Billy.

"Hey," he says.

"Hey," I say, almost tearfully relieved.

"What's happening, kid?"

He's peering into my face, his own face blending into the green hedge behind him.

"You all right?"

I have one hand on my chest, as if pledging allegiance to the flag.

"I don't know. I um, smoked too much—too much—with Pete and Ethan and these other . . ."—I pause to listen to my heart—". . . people.

"And, um, my heart—"

I look at Billy. Eyebrows raised, he's waiting to hear more. Apparently I haven't told him yet.

"Your heart," he says helpfully.

"It's beatin' . . ."

"It's beatin'?"

"Real fast."

"Your heart's beatin' real fast?"

"Yeah, Billy . . . my heart, it's beatin' *real fast.*"

"How much did you *smoke?*"

"I . . . don't know—a lot."

"What's 'a lot'?"

"Maybe seven—or even nine—joints."

"Seven or nine?" His eyes get big and he puffs out his cheeks, blowing out the air slowly.

I wait until he's done, until all the air's out, then add, "I think so." I push on the handlebars.

"Where you headed?"

"I gotta go home. I might . . . um . . . have to go to the hospital or something."

"Listen," he says, glancing over his shoulder. "That's probably not such a good idea."

"I don't know, Billy, I don't know—this is pretty bad." The bike won't move. Billy's holding it. I can't breathe again.

"I got a better idea," he's saying. After another minute he says, "Hey."

"What?" I say, hearing the edge of a sob in my voice.

"I got a better idea," he says. "Do you want to hear what it is?"

"Yeah."

He pivots the front wheel of my bike back in the direction of the ocean. "Just come out surfin'."

"No, I gotta go—"

"Trust me."

"But my heart!"

"Uh, let's not talk about your heart. Your heart's okay."

We begin to move. It's a cross between walking and floating painfully just above the street.

"Check it out," Billy says after a while. I look up into the sky where he's pointing above the trees. The tips sway. "Now that's what you call a full moon."

I'm already gazing at it, I realize now. Grainy light pours off in thin streams along the bottom. We're on the bottom, I think, the bottom of some kind of ocean. There's an ocean within the ocean.

"Okay." We've reached the edge of the road and the coast is clear to go across.

He climbs over the fence. I sit on the top railing for a bit, listening to my heart. A disembodied helmet of hair floats in the darkness: Billy's waiting for me. One of the people left in the circle calls his name, the word like a bat in the air.

Ethan and Pete are standing beside the broken fence, boards under their arms, looking at the waves.

"He's back," says Ethan.

After a while I look at the waves too. They gleam in the moonlight then break, closer to shore than before.

Pete delivers a karate kick to the fence.

Billy is talking to Ethan. The word "insane" blows past my head in the breeze.

Billy rubs the deck of his board with a piece of wax he's conjured out of thin air then says, "Ready?"

I move a little closer to look at the surf. Other members of the clique begin arriving in twos and threes now, their boards under their arms—as though it's morning instead of night—and we move down the slope of the beach, the boards lit in the moonlight.

I stop to check my heart but I can't hear it over the surf. White things blow across the sand—ghost crabs. I stand there watching them dart about until someone tugs me along by the arm.

Wading into the water, I overhear Billy, farther back up the beach, saying to someone in his version of my high, frightened voice, " . . . 'and my heart's beatin' *real fast!*' "

For a time, I seem to paddle in place, phosphorescent lines of white water crashing into and washing over me. Then I'm out.

I sit up on my board. The moonlight lies in a sheet to the horizon, glitters in the swirls around my legs, sparks along the edges of rills and boils left in the wake of the swells.

Off to one side, Billy pierces the taut back of a breaking wave, sits up on his board, spins and, without paddling, catches a wave peaking just behind it.

His head and the tip of the board flicker into view as he banks off the top, the spray like gravel from a fishtailing car.

Someone shouts, "All right, now!"

The cliff of a wave eclipses the moonlight. I lie down on my board, but gradually, in odd, thoughtful stages, wondering with detachment whether, moving so slowly, I'll be able to catch the wave when I finally begin to paddle, and then, paddling, being gathered up, fused to it, whether I'll manage to stand.

On my feet now, I hover at the peak for a long time, an hour, an afternoon, going nowhere, warm air flowing past the prow of my face. I'm a hood ornament.

Descending the face of the wave at last, the bottom of the board chatters across tiny, almost imperceptible ridges and bumps on the glassy surface.

At the bottom, I guide the board through a turn in what seems like extreme slow motion, rising back up the face, banking off the top and trimming.

As I turn again off the bottom and come, with a little burst of speed, to the end of the wave, someone hoots, and I notice three or four people watching me as they paddle out, the white foam of their boards gleaming.

The nearest one is Billy, drifting up the shoulder, his hands folded over the tip of his board. As our eyes meet, he grins at me.

I can't grin back. A mask of what feels like permanent seriousness has fallen over my face. But he was right. It's working. I can't hear my heart beating.

Which means that I won't die.

At home, the car's gone from the garage and so is Adam's bike. The wood paneling and sunlit, pragmatically furnished rooms seem flat and plain, like a barracks, after the ornate gloom of Carson's, where I've spent the night, but for that reason welcome too.

The sound of Mom's voice comes from the kitchen, its firm, wistful tone that of the "counselor" persona she adopts when advising one of her women friends.

She smiles and waves at me then goes back to doodling on a blank astrological wheel while listening on the phone. Jason's in his high chair beside her.

I fix myself a peanut butter and banana sandwich and eat it standing at the sink. I like listening to her side of the conversation, trying to piece together the other woman's sad problem. It's a kind of poetry.

"I thought we agreed that you weren't going to let that happen again," Mom says.

"I do. But I also know that this isn't healthy for either of you.

"It's just not.

"We've talked about why not.

"That's right.

"It may be—

"It—

"It may be time to consider that.

"One second, Janice." She covers the receiver and whispers, "The new *Surfer*'s here. It's on the coffee table."

"All right!"

I run water over my plate and dash into the living room, snatch up the *Surfer,* flop onto the couch and open it at random to a photo of Gerry Lopez, Mr. Pipeline.

"Jesus!"

The wave is massive, its lip like a jagged slab of blue ice, yet Lopez is standing nearly straight up in the tube, knees only slightly bent, arms limp, ho-hum. It's less like grace than sneer under pressure.

There seem to be two sorts of surfers: those who impose their will on a wave, and those who complement it. Of the latter type, Lopez is the epitome. Billy is this sort too. They brush the face with their fingers and find ways to linger until the tube enfolds them, remaining inside as long as possible. It's sensitive, this approach, intimate, fluid.

"Thad?" Mom calls.

Then there are the willful ones, the destroyers, like Nat Young, the Australian champ. I'm thinking of a *Surfer* cover shot leaving a flamethrower-like slash across the top of a large Hawaiian peak. Mike Tabeling, an East Coast big shot I recently saw at Sebastian Inlet, is in this camp. He's 6'8", Tabeling, but rode a tiny new design called a Fish. It was like watching a barbarian torch a village from atop a dwarf pony.

"Thad!"

I look up. She has the phone cradled on her shoulder and Jason on her knee now. "He needs his diaper changed!"

I nod but remain seated. Stalling or sighing like a martyr can sometimes exempt me from this smelly chore.

Which type am I? Well, for a while I considered myself more of the Lopez sort, but lately I've come to enjoy working up as much speed as possible. Which is not the same as imposing my will, but rather using the wave's dynamic. It's somewhere in between, I guess.

"Thad!"

"Coming!" I flip the *Surfer* so that it skids across the coffee table, pluck Jason from Mom's knee and take him out to the changing table on the patio. There are no fresh diapers in the drawer.

"We're out of diapers!"

She rises and goes back into the master bedroom.

I peer longingly through the living room windows at the *Surfer,* where it came to a halt on the edge of the coffee table. When a new one arrives, I commit the images and captions to memory by sheer repetition, read every article and finally, with a sense of desperation, the fine print of advertisements. At which point the pages have started to slip free of the binding and the sight of the issue makes me slightly ill.

Jason gurgles. His eyes are closed against the bright morning light and the tip of his tongue is poking out through his mouth, which turns down at the corners like Pat's. It's not only the mouth. He looks exactly like Pat—a tiny, helpless Pat, a Pat voodoo doll.

He clasps my thumb in his fist and squints at me. But he's half Mom too. And so, half me. Or is it a quarter me? Anyway, he's my brother. Which is more important, I think, than being a son. To be a brother is like being a fellow soldier, the way Adam and I are surviving together the war of being alive.

Jason will learn to swim soon. They should've started him already, before he knows enough to be afraid of the water. Then I'll teach him to surf. His hair will turn blond. Before long, he'll look more like me than Pat.

———

In the white sky, the football spins. I play end in the local league and, like any other boy in America, dream of the NFL. Only during the season, though, and while on land: from out in the ocean, football seems strange and perverse: all cleats on dried mud, shin splints, apoplectic faces.

But it's autumn and the waves are cold and bad, the color of broth. I'm playing catch with Adam and Clay, a boy from Tennessee. I envy his stocky build and speed.

The ball Clay has lofted strikes my palm and falls to the lawn. "Like a baby!"

It's Pat, home from work, his tie loosened.

"Catch it like you're catching a baby," he says. "Here."

Slowly, like the accumulation of data contradicting a prevailing worldview, a new model has been suggesting itself: Pat's not all bad. It's partly my having quit smoking pot, but mostly it's the son he hoists above his head and calls "Bambino!" He still blows up over trivial things, but less often. In the spring, he coached my baseball team. I'm his pitcher. We watch the Miami Dolphins together. He's telling me what he knows about sports.

I toss the ball. Pat catches it with a falling-away motion of his hands. "Go long."

I break down the grass past Adam and Clay, follow the ball as it plummets ahead of me and snag it with my fingertips.

"Nice hands!" Pat calls.

It fills me with pride.

Six

I n the ocean, a year dissolves like a streak of foam. It's August again, the water blue and flat as a table, though there is a small, promissory shore break and in it Adam and I roll like corpses, ears filled with the music of the shells dragged back and forth over the slope, the sound of treasure being sifted. It's the breathless middle of the day, crushingly hot. Eyes closed, we raise our heads above the surface, draw air and slip back under.

Since graduating from high school in June, Billy and company have been drifting quietly away. I hear the news from Ethan and Pete, who rent a small house Down South, leaning in the window of their gray Dart at the Ocean Avenue boardwalk. They stop there to check the surf and smoke a joint before waiting tables at Poor Richards, white tuxedo shirts open at their brown throats.

Billy is the one I miss, the one to whom my thoughts turn now. It was inevitable, his immigration to Hawaii, like rising to heaven, though instead of the North Shore of Oahu, he went to Kauai. It's overcrowded on the North Shore, frantic with ambition, and the violence of the locals is legendary: Jeff Crawford, the first Floridian to ride Pipeline with real flair, had a can of dog food smashed into his face. Billy is too refined for all of that.

I'm not. I want it all: the light at the top, on the cover of *Surfer,* the light around the winner of the Duke Kahanamoku

Classic on the *Wide World of Sports* as he says a few humble words into the microphone.

Pushing off the ledge into an astronaut's slow somersault, I see again how fame will come: a peak the size of an alp draws me up its face, while all along shore, photographers bow at the waist like butlers and peer into their viewfinders.

I climb out of the water and trot up the beach for my board. Beginning today, if there are no waves, I will paddle a mile.

"Hey!" Adam is sitting up facing shore. He must have felt my absence underwater. Foam from a wavelet pours past his neck like an ermine collar.

"What're you doing?"

"Training."

I set the board in the water. "I'm gonna paddle to stay in shape."

"I need to stay in shape too!"

I climb on the board and point the nose north, arms slung in the warm water. Adam paddles up alongside me. We squint into the blinding distance.

"How far?"

"To the boardwalk. That's a mile."

It's not a random destination. The boardwalk means Phil Meta. On the wall of Darcy's hangs a framed photograph of him shaking hands with the Duke. It was taken the year Meta represented the East Coast in the Duke Kahanamoku Classic.

The sun presses its hand on our backs. It's harder than it seems, paddling so far. Sargasso weed lies in brown clumps on the sand, like roadkill, fed on by tiny flies; the houses along the bluff seem abandoned. Slicked back, our hair dries in a streak then springs upward like a dorsal spine.

My shoulder blades ache, cramp. Adam slips behind. Sitting up to rest, I see him walking back along the beach through wavering lines of heat.

I would quit too, but I've made a promise: I will paddle one mile. I take such things seriously. I must have self-discipline. What would I be without it? Just one of the boys.

As I near the boardwalk, something strange happens: the mild pleasure of my crotch pressed against the board intensifies, liquifies, spreads through me like sap. I feel it in my hands, in my fingertips. It's like a possession, though I suppose it's only what I've heard about—puberty.

The beach is lined with sunbathers here. I float in the water with my elbows on the deck of the board and wait for the erection to subside. It takes a long time, and when I finally walk up onto the sand, I shield my crotch with the nose of the board in case there's a resurgence.

Three years have passed since I first came here. The crowd along the boardwalk is thinner and blander now. The spider monkeys and greasepaint are no more. Instead there are tourists in white hats, arms bright as slapped faces.

A health-food bar has replaced the head shop. I have enough for a small carrot juice. With sea-pickled fingers, I unstick coins from a bar of Sex Wax and hand them to one of the beautiful women. She scrapes at a nickel with her thumbnail, makes a face and drops it in the register.

In Darcy's, Meta leans on the circular laminated counter like a bartender, phone cradled against his ear. If he were an animal he would be an orangutan, though a handsome one, with a prominent nose and sly, intelligent eyes. I take him in with shy glances. He has a bad back and surfs stiffly now. I've seen him out at the boardwalk a number of times. His shoulder blades are pitted with acne scars.

When he notices me at the rack of boards, Meta gives a little wave. Sometimes he remembers my name, otherwise he calls me "Kid." Yet as I dawdle away afternoons here, he discloses things: that he's never tried LSD, for instance, though he would consider taking it on a sunny day in Hawaii. I remember everything he says, especially the tone. I mull the words over like the lyrics of a ballad I'm composing.

As in the movies, he gets off the phone without saying good-bye. "There he is."

"Hey."

"See anything you like?"

"This is hot," I say, tilting a yellow board out of its slot. I'm not sure why I think so, but then all the boards are made in Meta's factory in Melbourne, so it's hard to go wrong complimenting one of them.

"Yep," he agrees. "What're you riding these days?"

"Six foot three, round pin."

"One of mine?"

"Oh yeah," I say, imitating Carson. He's in Los Angeles at his father's.

Meta purses his lips. "Check out the red one down the line there."

"This?"

"Yeah. Nice, no?"

"Wow, yeah."

I wish I could think of a natural way to bring up the contest victories. I've entered two sponsored by the Eastern Surfing

Association and won them both. There were only three of us in the Boy's Division, and Adam was one (he came in third). But the trophies are real enough. I've consecrated a shelf in my room to them—and to the ones to follow.

The bells on the door tinkle. A burly man wearing mirrored shades and a dark walrus mustache shoulders into the shop and spreads his arms like an impresario. Of Meta's cronies, I've noticed two kinds: surfers, and shady types like this guy.

"Mai Tai!" he bellows.

"Well, well," Meta says.

The man looks around then reaches up as if to bring down a big-wave board hung above the door like an ancient weapon. "That's the one I need! Think I'm ready, Phil?"

"Ready to drown," Meta says. "Hey," he adds. "We need to get on Jack's case about Miami."

"Phil," the man says in a disappointed tone. He's pressing a wet suit to his chest like a dress, as if to gauge the fit. "Let me ask you something: what do we really know about Jack?"

Meta pauses to think. "Jack shit, really."

"Exactly."

"So?"

"So nothing. We wait."

Here they fall silent, as if unwilling to say more in my presence. I can take a hint.

"I'm gonna hit it, Phil."

"Okay. Take it easy, Thad."

He remembered!

"See that kid?" Meta says as the door closes. "He's going to be big one day." Or so I imagine.

———————

In Melbourne Beach, the ocean is relatively murky, but one day, as if a drop of elixir has fallen into it, the water turns clear from top to bottom. Word spreads and everyone brings snorkeling gear to the beach. I'm swimming along the sand at a depth of ten feet when something makes me look toward the deep, far out, beyond any lineup, where the color runs to a terrible blue and I can never gaze for long. It's the Other Side, the Realm of Death.

Out of it soars a manta ray with the wingspan of a hang glider. I'm unafraid, or almost unafraid. I stare through the hooked mandibles into the cavern of its body. The vent-like gills on its white underbelly ripple. It seems to look back at me.

Then it banks like a spaceship and disappears into the blue.

———————

Bracketed from this life, and dream-like, are the annual visits to Washington, usually in August, when the city's car fumes are sealed beneath a dome of humidity.

I pack grumpily. I've long ago lost all interest in museums and zoos and pet shops, the only places Dad thinks to take me. Walking on so much concrete makes my legs sore, the pollution gives me headaches.

"You live in a terrarium down there!" he remarked last summer, as though Florida had unfit me for real life. Maybe it has.

As the plane pierces the dazzling white of a slowly boiling cloud and banks north over the Atlantic, I look longingly at the water. It's the beginning of hurricane season. I'm vexed by the possibility of missing waves, incurring the slightest loss of fluency in my surfing. But at this point it's also the paltriness of the arrangement: one week per year? Why bother at all?

Hours later, I spot Dad waiting at my gate, in the sudden density of people that means the city. Smiling, he waves and moves forward. It's more exciting to see him than I've allowed myself to imagine it would be, and I feel a twinge of shame for my coldness. Isn't he doing the best he can?

This year, instead of hugging, we shake hands. I'm thirteen, nearly six feet tall and dizzy with the inches I've grown. My hands knock over glasses at the dinner table, my moods change like the channels of a TV capriciously switched.

He's moved from an apartment downtown to a split-level house on a tree-lined street tucked along a ridge of Rock Creek Park.

I stand in the driveway and sniff the air. There seems to be more oxygen here. I put my suitcase in the guest room and he shows me around.

There's the piano inherited from his musician parents, Chopin on the music stand, cabinets and dishes from Poland. Memories of things I've lost sight of in the furnace of light and water, dimmer, civilized things reappear: being in the college bell tower with my grandfather while he played the keyboard. Harsh things too: the older cousin who fawned before the adults, then, when we were alone, lashed my legs with an oak branch.

I leaf through photo albums, lift a lizard tchotchke from the coffee table. "I remember this!"

"You do, eh?"

Two years ago he married a former student, Corinne, a tall, dark-haired beauty eleven years his junior who's studying for a PhD in French literature now. Half French, half American, she grew up in Paris and came to the States for college. We'll have lunch at her parents' apartment, swim in the pool with retired diplomats and afterward drink Coke served with a slice of lemon.

We hear her come in downstairs, toss keys into a dish in the foyer. "Hello! Is that who I think it is?" We've grown fond of each other.

Theirs is a world of books, trips to Italy and Greece, dinner-table arguments about politics amid fragrant cigarette smoke. It's refined but wan, like their skin, and I pity them slightly.

———

Wild Kingdom is on, the voice of Marlin Perkins commenting with senescent cheer as his young partner, in the coils of an anaconda, is jerked beneath the surface of a muddy river.

"When I grow up," Adam declares, "I'm gonna live in a tree." He's been making this announcement for years.

"You can't just live in a tree," Pat says.

"Why not?"

Pat takes a sip of his coffee. "Somebody owns that tree." The seriousness with which he takes this debate always surprises me.

"Not in the jungle."

"The jungle is just part of some country. The government owns it."

"In the middle of the jungle? You can't own the jungle!"

"Of course you can."

"Pat," Mom calls from the kitchen, "he can live in a tree if he wants to."

"Yeah," Adam says, folding his arms. "There are parts of the jungle where no one's even *been* yet."

Pat smirks. "Okay, Tarzan. Let's say you're right. What are you going to eat up there in your tree?"

"Bananas and stuff."

"Bananas and stuff."

"The tree has everything you need right there in it!"

"What about when it rains? Are you going to just sit up in your tree shivering in the rain?"

It's Adam's turn to smirk. "The rain is *warm* in the jungle."

"Yeah, all right," Pat says, waving his hand in disgust. "Warm rain, free bananas."

They lapse into a grudging silence.

Who is right? I picture Adam in his tree, Pat in an office with the deed to the land.

Chins set, frowning, they are like a riddle: one small and light, the other big and dark, yet the same—thinking about the tree.

———

One night that autumn, Carla, a girl in the class ahead of me, coasts up on her bike while I'm shooting baskets in our driveway. Pat and Mom have gone out to dinner, Adam's inside watching Jason. Carla has a round pale face, lips often pursed to conceal crooked teeth and fine brown hair she is either brushing nervously or raking her fingers through. It swings from side to side when she walks.

She's talking as she rides up—"Oh my God, can you even see the basket?"—and keeps talking until something shifts in the air between us and we kiss.

I lean her against Pat's tool bench and slip my hand up under her halter top. To my surprise, she takes me in her fist through my tennis shorts.

"You have a big Oscar Meyer!"

Having looked around at the other boys in the gym shower, I'm flooded with happiness at this unexpected news.

But car lights are bouncing onto the back wall of the garage and I send her through the house to avoid detection by Pat and Mom.

A few days later, riding bikes, we spot each other in the distance and go back to Carla's house.

She knows about sex, she explains, from her older sisters and from books—there's a stack of them, pamphlet-like, on the kitchen table—given to her by her mother.

"And who," Carla's saying, "could come home any second, so—"

"So?" I say, pushing her onto her bed. She squeezes me in her hand again and says, out of breath, "So—we need to keep our ears, um, pricked, ha, ha!"

We take off each other's clothes—I'm wearing only a pair of baggies.

"Hello, Oscar Meyer! Forget it, you're not going there with it, now be a good boy—Margaret Mead says the reason kids in the Tropics have sex so young—is that door locked?—hey,

you be good, I said no—is because of the heat—check the door
and come straight back here, fox—was it locked?—you've never
heard of Margaret Mead, have you? God, I love dumb surfers!
She's a famous anthropologist, you ignoramus. She thinks—
oh shit, wait, was that the garage door?—Thad, I'm totally
kidding, I don't think you're an ignoramus—she thinks that
kids in the Tropics have sex so young because of the heat
and running around half naked like you. The heat makes
them go through puberty—oh shit, that was definitely the
garage door—she's back, she's back! Here, here—out the
window!"

I pull on my baggies and hop through the open window,
landing in a hedge with a crunch and cutting my foot.

"I'll call you!"

That night the phone rings. Pat passes it to me.

I can hear her speaking before the receiver reaches my
ear.

"—and my mother saw your bike!"

"Yeah?"

She laughs. "You don't give a shit, do you?"

I don't, but not because I'm brave. I just don't care about
Carla, I'm not sure why.

"Well, maybe you'll give a shit about what I'm about to tell
you."

"What's that?"

"Are you sitting down?"

"Yeah." I'm standing at the kitchen counter flipping through
a *Sports Illustrated*.

"Okay. I've decided to lose my virginity to you."

"Really?"

"Yes, really," Carla says. "Would I kid about something like that?"

"Wow."

"This is a very big deal, you know."

"Uh—I know."

"Do you? I mean, I'll never forget you, not for the rest of my life. That's how it is for girls. When a girl gives her virginity, she remembers the guy forever. Because it's unique."

She pauses as if to encourage me to say something.

"I just thought you should know that. So you're very special—that's all."

She pauses again.

"When?" I ask finally.

"Oh my God! 'When,' he says! Oh my God! Whoa, boy! Easy, tiger!"

———

Carson lets us use his living room, then keeps a watch at the front window.

We sit beside each other on the couch. When I reach for her, Carla pins my hand to a cushion. "Do you know anything about foreplay?"

"Sure."

"Like I believe you! Anyway, there's this thing, I read about it, it's called the 'spoon game.'"

She fishes around in her purse and pulls out a spoon. "A girl needs foreplay to come. Boys come at the drop of a hat."

She puts the spoon on her ankle and then my hand on the spoon. "Try to pass it up the leg of my pants, like this. Try to sort of move the spoon upward," she says, her voice thickening.

"Carla, we don't have much time."

"All right already!" She unzips her jeans and has wiggled them down to her thighs when Carson runs in.

"You guys, the Colonel's home!"

He sweeps aside the curtains to the patio and opens the sliding-glass door. "This way, quick!"

————

Then the Phillips' parents go out to dinner and we hastily arrange to meet at their house, a large one built on the crest of the beach. When they moved here from Miami two years ago, the eldest son, who's fourteen, took up surfing, and now Carson and I stash our boards in their backyard. Carla knows the sons and their little sister, and has somehow become friends with the mother, a housewife who wears cat's-eye glasses and has decorated the wood-paneled walls of the house with nets strung with scallop shells.

Standing at a window on the second floor, I see Carla ride up the long driveway on her bike.

The little sister appears beside me. "She's coming! She's coming!"

Carson is in the living room with the Phillips brothers and Clay. Everyone is privy.

I hear Carla talking to them, then her clogs on the stairs.

"Oh, hi, Thad!" she says. "Fancy meeting you here!"

"Hi, Carla."

"Uh, Thad, could I talk to you for a second?"

"How about in here?"

She closes the door of the guest room behind her. We hear everyone burst into giggles downstairs.

"My reputation is never going to recover from this."

"They're cool," I say.

"But you're hot."

I pull her toward the narrow bed.

"Hold your horses, tiger." She fishes around in her purse and comes up with a spoon. "Look, I brought it."

She's wearing hot pants. Panting lightly, she sits on the edge of the bed and puts the spoon on the white skin of her thigh.

"Give it a try," she says.

I sit next to her and put one hand on the spoon and with the other I tug at the button of her shorts. It pops open, the spoon falls to the carpet and Carla grabs me through my baggies.

"Oh well!" she says, and in another few seconds we're out of our clothes.

"Now at least go slow!" she hisses. "The main thing is to go slow!"

Lying back on the sofa as I lower myself over her, she looks frightened.

"Promise me."

"Okay," I say thickly. "I will."

"Stop if I say, okay?"

"Yeah, okay."

"'Yeah, okay.' Oh my God, I don't know about this!"

I lower myself onto her again.

"Here, wait."

From her purse she takes a small jar of Vaseline, scoops out a dollop with two fingers then smears it over the head of my penis and I nearly come. The petroleum scent of the Vaseline mixes with the smells of sex. Carla lies back down, I mount her. It slides in, the sensation like fire.

Carla says, "Wait—it hurts!"

A droplet of my sweat splashes on her collarbone.

I pull out.

"Okay—go.

"Wait—stop!

"Okay—go.

"Stop. Okay.

"There. Ouch. God.

"Wait! It hurts."

I pull back out.

"This hurts too much. Stop!

"Okay—go."

Now I'm all the way in.

I push once, twice, thrice.

"I'm starting!" Carla cries. "I'm starting!"

But so am I.

Eighth grade in the large mediocre junior high school in Indialantic: "portable" cabin classrooms baking in the sun atop cinder blocks, glimpses of weary teachers sipping coffee from Styrofoam cups in the sanctuary of their lounge and the tedium of the whole routine occasionally broken by a mildly retarded boy who shouts, "It's bal-loooooooon time!"

There's no ethnicity here: the sun's bleaching and tanning effects unify us, and the community is too rootless and All-American Space Age for such distinctions. Race exists in the form of three black students but is almost never mentioned. Class also has little if any meaning yet, though occasionally Carson will draw my attention to it.

There's a Pakistani boy, for instance, the son of a doctor, who surfs in front of his house at Seawall, next to Billy's beach. He attends boarding school and, because he keeps pointedly to himself, Carson and I have come to see him in a tragic light, as though privilege has enisled him in solitude.

I have a crush on a girl of this sort: Alice Choate. Mysterious and refined, with slightly crossed almond eyes and thick hair worn in a bun, she lives in a big house on the river and has, though I'm not sure what it means, New England roots. Instead of going to the beach when school lets out, she makes paintings and ceramics under the tutelage of Mrs. Guillaume, the brittle art teacher, then rides home on an old-fashioned bike, the pedals turning slowly.

I've served a detention for acting up in English class and now, on my way out of the building, I make a point of passing the studio. Alice, her back to the door, is bent over one of the long tables, arranging the tesserae of a mosaic, the hum of the fluorescent lights like a Gregorian chant. I wish I still drew, and not merely as a way to insinuate myself into her consciousness. I miss the serene reliability of pen, paper and lamplight.

I read—books about baseball, fishing, shark attacks, biographies of sports figures, the occasional novel. But at home. In school I can't sit still when there might be waves—which is anytime, all the time.

One day her younger sister passes me a note: "Alice likes you."

"Really?" We're talking after class. The sister is wiry and animated.

"Yes! My God, haven't you noticed how she stares at you?"

I have, but I never dared hope that it might mean this. If I can desire from afar someone as rarefied as Alice Choate and then, as in a fairy tale, be desired in return, what wonders might be possible?

But the school year's almost over and we've yet to speak to each other. We share no classes, and in the halls she's usually flanked by a pair of girlfriends who radiate disapproval of me. The entire school knows about Carla, so maybe it's that.

There are now only a few days left before summer break and Alice Choate is slipping away. Since our love is apparently above small talk, I decide to sweep aside all such petty preliminaries, stride boldly up and kiss her. That done, we can get down to the business of being girlfriend and boyfriend.

I disclose the plan to no one, not even Carson. I might lose my nerve. Between classes I cruise the banks of lockers like a shark circling a reef. Twice I go to do it and a teacher turns the corner or one of her friends appears and I veer away.

Finally, a crowd of students parts like a school of fish and I see Alice alone. She's spinning the dial of her lock.

I walk over quickly and she turns to me with her habitual expression, that of a mildly perplexed hauteur, the very look that has made it so hard to speak to her. But I'm overstepping all that now, leaning to kiss her.

Her eyes widen, and as she opens her mouth to say something my lips meet her braces.

Pushing me back with both hands, she says, "What are you *doing?*"

Me? Doing?

From somewhere nearby the retarded boy shouts, "It's bal-loooooon time!"

I shrug idiotically and walk off, the world a roaring passageway I navigate by instinct until I've walked down a hall and out of the building. Sunlight winks on the chrome of the bikes parked in the racks. I press a knuckle to my mouth and the skin is marbled by blood.

I ride home, change into my baggies, then slide my board from the rack on the patio. Adam's in the yard, tossing underhanded over and over a white plastic ball to Jason, who wears a baseball uniform Mom made for him and swings with an orange plastic bat. They're inseparable.

"It's no good!" Adam calls.

I ride my bike to the beach. The waves are small, but there are waves. No one else is out.

I wade into the shore break. The water is warm and the milky green it often turns in the afternoon. I paddle; a line of soup washes over me, then another. The crust of shame begins to dissolve, though the taste of the rubber and metal of her braces lingers.

———

The best TV is *Hawaii Five-O*, though really only the wave in the introductory sequence, that monstrous omnivorous left, the clip of which lasts a few heartbeats but elicits groans of terror and awe or, if Adam or I say anything, it's something like "No!" or "Oh my *God!*"

If Pat's out of earshot: "Oh my *fucking God!*"

The wave is riderless and looks unridable, but the theme music, the stirring rumble of the drums and heroic pump of the brass, compels us to imagine attempting to ride it—hence the groans. Then it's gone and we're bereft.

When the surf has been bad, it can seem as if the *Hawaii Five-O* wave is the only real one, that compared to it there are no waves at all here. And I wonder: is Florida unreal because it's not Hawaii? Am I a real surfer even though I'm in Florida? When am I finally going to be in Hawaii? I wished to move to Florida and we did. Now I wish to move to Hawaii but we're still in Florida. Why?

But when the surf has been good, the *Hawaii Five-O* wave can seem like little more than TV. Seeing the same wave over and over renders it and Hawaii unreal, something dreamed up in Hollywood, like fake earthquakes or Mr. Ed, the talking horse.

The show itself is tiresome, the moral always: paradise lost. But every so often the plot involves the ocean or a surfer or simply a boat with a cargo of drugs bobbing on the breast of the Pacific, so we watch it loyally. It's really all there is. Once a year, the Duke Kahanamoku Classic is covered by the *Wide World of Sports,* but *Hawaii Five-O* winks at us weekly, and otherwise, as surfers, we don't exist on TV.

The break at nearby Avenue B is distinguished by a small circle of older surfers, a few in their fatherly thirties, like Billy and company aged and winnowed. They make boards for a living, mostly in Meta's factory, working as shapers, glassers, glossers or sanders.

If none is quite of star magnitude, all surf with enormous polish, dominating in the local E.S.A. contests. They also have wives and girlfriends so interchangeable in their willowy white-blond perfection that I've begun to wonder whether such a beauty won't one day simply materialize and take my arm.

The most famous figure is Stan Dryden, a sander by trade and, as *Surfer's* East Coast photographer, a kind of kingmaker. Wearing a sour expression, he sits astride his board in the afternoon chop, fiberglass dust powdering his long brown hair like a periwig.

Adam and I are paddling past. I'm wary of looking at Dryden directly. The last thing I want is to jeopardize my future with any presumptuous familiarity.

But it was actually Adam who discovered this world—through his friend Joshua, the son of the shaper Ed Hodge—and at some point, he has assumed the role of mascot.

"Hey, Stan!" he chirps now.

With a mixture of amazement and annoyance, I watch as Dryden's mustache lifts crookedly in a rare smile and he waves. Though the wave includes me too, I suppose. But am I merely "Adam's older brother"?

Later, I'm mooning around in my usual way at Darcy's when Meta gets off the phone. "Want a summer job?"

People—beginners or dabblers for the most part—sometimes leave their boards at Darcy's to be repaired, and the surfer who patches dings in the factory has yet to come back from a trip to Barbados. Meta's tossing it to me like a scrap, but there's a gleam in his eyes. He must know what this means.

"Definitely, Phil!" I say. "Definitely!"

What I don't say is that I don't really know how to patch dings—not with the finish expected of factory work, at least.

"I'll have Dryden swing by and pick you up in the morning. Wait outside at seven."

"Great!"

I sail home on my bike. The huge pines sigh. The world is open, radiant, the pages of the future fanning, gilt-edged, in the sky. There can be no doubt of it: I'm being apprenticed to greatness.

Now it's early morning on Friday. I'm on the curb gazing steadily up the street at the corner Dryden's car will turn when he comes for me—if he ever does. Yesterday he either forgot or didn't go to work.

Finally, like the sun returning after an eclipse, the orange Toyota station wagon appears in the distance. I jump to my feet.

Riding shotgun is Tim Miller, a thin blond whose speciality is pinstripes.

Dryden pulls over. I open the door and hesitate. T-shirts and jeans, wadded and covered in fiberglass dust, lie across the seat.

Glancing back, Dryden says, "Just slide that shit over."

I sit attentively, a court secretary prepared to record the least bit of gossip or wisdom. But Miller seems to be sleeping, and other than saying, as he passes an old man on a bike, "Pedal it all the way to Tampa, gramps!," Dryden drives in a grouchy silence.

Finally, in a bleak, unfamiliar part of Melbourne, Miller perks up. "There's one, Stan!"

Dryden pulls onto the shoulder and Miller jogs back to a telephone pole. Looking around nervously, he jerks something down and runs back to the car with it clutched to his chest. Dryden peels out.

It's a cardboard poster advertising upcoming appearances of black musicians posed in ruffled dress shirts.

"T-Bone and the Five Steps!" Miller reads aloud. "The Soul Searchers! The Ravens!"

"All right!" says Dryden.

What they find so funny about the poster I have no idea—something subtle and sophisticated, no doubt.

Dryden says, "So I was over at Loehr's the other day?"

I lean forward. Greg Loehr is a young surf star who has been appearing in *Surfer,* thanks to Dryden. I had the privilege of watching him at the boardwalk once. His approach is coiled, precise and violent, organized around blade-like, vertical swipes.

"Have you ever looked in his closet? It's like someone took everything"— Dryden raises both arms—"and went ugh!" He brings his arms down abruptly. "Shit just everywhere."

"He's a slob all right," Miller concurs affectionately.

As I mull over this inside dope, Dryden steers down a dirt road and into the weedy lot behind a two-story building. A truck and two cars, one of them Ed Hodge's, are parked beside a dusty locust tree.

"No way out now!" Dryden mutters. He's tying his hair up into a ponytail, knotting it. I follow them across the yard.

"It's payday, don't forget," Miller says.

"Forget? I'm obsessed."

Around the door are snarls of masking tape, fried-chicken buckets half full of hardened resin.

The interior has been divided into work spaces by walls of Sheetrock. From somewhere comes the whine of an electric planer.

Dryden pulls on a white dust mask, slams a James Brown eight-track tape into a stereo, turns the volume up—"Get Down stole my girlfriend/That ain't right!"—and stalks down a hall, from which direction there momentarily emanates the shriek of an electric sander.

Miller staples the R&B poster up beside ten or so others on a wall.

"That's you," he says, nodding toward a rack of about twenty boards, a shelf bearing jars of pigment and resin, and a board stand.

I try to think of a question that won't expose my ignorance, but he's already disappeared around a corner.

What now? I inspect the boards, looking for something easy. The dings range from rail gouges and punctures to fractures and water-logged sections where the fiberglass has delaminated, pulled itself free of the foam. One board's snapped in two, the halves attached only by strands of fiberglass.

With growing dread, I select a blue board with a rail gouge, lay it on the stand, then, folding up a square of sandpaper, buff tentatively at the ding and tape off the area with masking tape.

Toby, Matt, Carson—everyone I know is better at this. I not only have no aptitude for it, I've been cultivating a fantasy of remaining above the practical realm of surfing, like a race-car driver to his pit crew. But that's a pipe dream. Even Loehr works making boards somewhere, I'd bet. Well, maybe not Loehr. He's probably supported by surf companies, or wealthy patrons who love great surfing. But until I get as good as he is, I'll have to learn the crafts here, even if it means teaching myself.

Meanwhile, a sort of sleepy hopelessness, as in math class, is stealing over me. I squat beside a stack of *Surfers*, flip through a few issues. My photos will appear here before long. It's guaranteed now, like a scholarship or inheritance that's been set aside for me.

I wander to the bathroom with an issue, read for a while, then follow the whine of a planer down a long hallway and peek in through a gap in the Sheetrock.

Inside is Ed Hodge, Joshua's father, wearing a filter mask and pacing alongside a blank. The planer sends up a rooster tail of foam powder. He's covered in it. He has short reddish hair and a bull-like, choleric look—a sort of ruddy Pat.

He crouches and runs the flat of his hand down the deck of the blank. His eyes above the mask are fearsome and I decide to leave before he catches me spying on him.

I plod reluctantly back to my station and stare at the blue board.

"There he is."

It's Meta's glasser, Tyler Schwartz, eating a peach. Beside him in the doorway is Jim, his wise-looking mutt.

"Hey, Tyler! Have you been here all this time?"

Tyler is the kindest of the Avenue B circle and Adam's favorite. He'll help me.

"Just got in," he says.

He has sad brown eyes, smooth walnut skin and fine brown hair brushed with gold. In fact, he resembles nothing so much as the little picture of Jesus he glasses onto the decks of his boards (so that the image is pressed to his heart when he's paddling). He never proselytizes, though come to think of it, Adam has been reading the Bible lately. His convictions find expression mainly in a certain melancholy tinging his manner, the lonely way he strokes Jim's fur, the chastened fluidity of his surfing.

He takes a last bite of the peach, replaces the James Brown tape with Neil Young's *Harvest* and looks through the rack of dinged boards. "Finding your way around?"

"I guess so," I say morosely, grimacing at the board on the stand. "I don't know."

"You'll get it wired eventually." He inspects the ding. I look over his shoulder.

"Um, you might want to build this up a bit," he suggests gently, pointing to the tape. "So it'll catch more of the resin, and—"

He takes the roll in his teeth and tears off a few strips, applying them to the board with deft, confident swipes. "And form the rail, you know, like this?"

A few minutes later he's patched the blue board and set up three others, so that essentially all I need to do is pour the resin and sand them down once they've dried.

"Damn," I say, causing a wince of disapproval to appear on his face. "Thanks, Tyler!"

"Anytime," he says. "I'll be right down the hall if you need me."

"Great!"

At noon, Miller collects money from everyone and comes back with subs. We sit on crates near the back door: Hodge, Schwartz, Miller, Dryden and a man named Talbot, who does the glossing.

Meta's orange van barrels into the yard. The burly man I've seen at Darcy's is in the passenger seat, mirrored shades on.

"Payday," Miller says.

"We're *rich*," says Dryden.

Meta swaggers up, grinning in the dusty sunlight. "Howdy, boys!"

"Howdy, Sheriff!" says Dryden.

Meta passes out the paychecks. "How's the rookie doin'?"

"Okay," I tell him.

He glances at the work under way in my area, thrusts out his lower lip. "Lookin' good."

He has each of the others show him where they are in the production line and drives off.

At three o'clock, work is stopped for the day. I get a ride back to the beach with Hodge. He stops at a drive-through bank to cash his paycheck for three hundred dollars. I've never seen so much money.

Driving away, he tosses it into the air like a child playing in a pile of autumn leaves. It's exhilarating.

"This is all gonna be worthless in two years!"

"Yeah?"

"It's shit!" He scatters the cash contemptuously around the front seat. "The economy is on the verge of total collapse."

A few twenties have fallen to the floor at my feet.

"Shit!" he shouts merrily.

The next morning I find Pat at the kitchen table reading the paper. "Looks like your friend got busted."

"Who?"

"Phil Meta."

He passes me the paper. There at the bottom of the front page is a brief article about it: Meta was arrested after trying to sell a large quantity of marijuana to an undercover agent.

I'm not exactly shocked. But what does Pat make of this? Surfing doesn't interest him like football and baseball, but it's a sport, and therefore wholesome in his eyes. Is he going to think I'm involved in some sort of drug ring?

He takes a sip of coffee and says, not unsympathetically, "So much for the summer job, I guess, huh?"

"Maybe not. I mean, the factory might stay open."

"Not if he goes to prison."

He goes to prison.

———————

Neal and Nellie come from Tampa each summer to visit Pat. Barbie-doll cute and difficult to impress, Nellie watches TV and languidly practices gymnastic moves on the lawn. Neal, on the other hand, has grown into a delinquent, and is suddenly in so much trouble that his mother declares that he either live here with us or be remanded to a juvenile home.

I watch him come up the driveway. He's thin to the point of gaunt and walks with his elbows cocked. The suitcase seems to jerk him along with its weight.

He wants to learn to surf. If anything can save him, it's surfing. I believe this. As soon as he's settled into his room, I make him a gift of one of my old boards.

We paddle out toward evening, the waves a summer wind swell, the sort that crowds itself, leaping suddenly like chop.

I stay by Neal's side, coaching him. I try to see through his eyes, and it's dizzying: so much ambiguous information lapping, flickering.

A small wave rises up before us.

"Try this one," I tell him.

Awkwardly he paddles a half circle, looks back over his shoulder.

"No, wait, never mind," I decide. "It's not going to break."

Later, I see him catch and ride his first wave, knock-kneed and shaky but determined. There's a sort of flash around the moment, as the energy of the wave, alive and electrical beneath him, is sent outward in a burst. He trims the board and stays on his feet until the end. He'll be good if he can stay with it.

I hoot and paddle over to him. "Nice wave!"

"Wow," he says, grinning, teeth and eyeballs aglow in the dusk.

"Pretty cool, huh?"

"Amazing!"

At home, Adam announces, "Neal rode his first wave!"

Pat smiles. "You did, eh?"

Neal grins. "Yep!"

"That's great, Neal!" Mom says. "That is so great!"

Returning the favor, Neal teaches me to drive the Volvo stick shift. But when the surf goes flat, the prospect of playing dead in the shore break bores Neal. He finds other forms of amusement for us. We pelt cars on A1A, using juice oranges, are caught and made to apologize at the police station. We torment the fat girl who baby-sits Jason then sit on the couch while a disgusted Mom and Pat lecture us.

The waves return in September but Neal is preoccupied with high school social life. His new friends don't surf. When he speaks to them on the phone, he lowers his voice and turns away from me. Report cards turn out to be doctored, official mail intercepted.

"Neal, goddammit!" Pat calls for him. Their confrontations

grow more frequent. One day there's a crashing noise out in the garage and Neal, holding his jaw, stalks into the house and back to his room. Did Pat strike him?

In December he's trying to dry out a pound of green pot by baking it in the oven when Pat comes home unexpectedly.

Adam and I tiptoe to the bathroom.

"Did you do it?" Pat says.

There's a silence, though Neal must nod because Pat shouts, "Then admit it!

"*Act like a man!*" he growls.

Act like a man! we tease Neal later.

But not for long: he's shipped back to Tampa.

———

Red flags flutter in an onshore breeze, marking the contest area at the north end of the boardwalk. Early spring, mid-afternoon sunlight plates the moving surface of the waves. The air is ablur with marine blues and sea spray.

I glance back at the crest of the beach, where the judge's table has been set up, and pick out Meta's silhouette. Word is he was released from prison two weeks ago.

A banner behind and above the table, held upright by bamboo poles stuck into the sand, reads FIRST ANNUAL HOOVER JUNIOR HIGH SCHOOL SURFING CONTEST SPONSORED BY DARCY'S SURF SHOP. On the boardwalk are Pat, Mom in her white tennis hat and sunglasses, holding Jason, and Adam, his helmet of hair flaring in the light when he turns his head.

I wax my board, scribbling the bar in tight circles, then put the nub in the pocket of my baggies and look around at the four other finalists.

With Matt Thyme in Eleuthera and Toby somehow eliminated in the semifinals, my only competition is Tommy Stoltz, younger brother of Jim, one of the Billy Olin crew.

He senses my gaze and turns to me with a shy grin. We like each other. He hasn't surfed as long as I have, but has been improving fast, how much I'm not sure, since we usually surf at different beaches now. He's small and I worry that he'll fare better in the dropping, somewhat feeble surf.

Someone touches my shoulder. It's Carson, in tennis clothes. He's grown tall and slim.

"How'd you do?" I ask.

"Second round." Carson shrugs.

He competes in tournaments around the state, rarely advancing very far. The competition is ferocious. He shouts when he hits the ball.

The horn blares.

"Good luck, man!" he says softly.

"Thanks."

"I'll be watching you rip."

I jog into the water with the others.

Once through the shore break, I sit up and take my bearings. The waves breaking on the outside bar look weak and inconsistent, the shore break smaller and inclined to close out. Why didn't I study this when I was sitting on the beach?

The heat is twenty minutes long, but I lost my watch in the water a few days ago. A band of white skin encircles my wrist. It's beginning to blister.

Glancing back at the crowd of students arrayed on the beach, the banner and judges' table, I feel dizzy and leaden.

I roll off my board and into the water to clear my head, then climb on and sprint-paddle to the outside bar, moving to and fro in the lineup until finally, more glitter than color, a wave stands up and I catch it and ride, winding back and forth like a snake, working it into the middle break, where it dies and I kick out, calmer now.

Turning to paddle back to the outside, I see Tommy sliding into a steep shore-break peak, arms drawn back with the speed of the descent. I hesitate, then decide to surf the inside too.

The rest of the heat is an adrenalized blur: off-the-tops mistimed, the lip crashing into my thighs, waves caught and ridden hastily, in a kind of panic, the board slipping from my hands as I kick out, then galloping through the shallows for it and turning to see Tommy squeeze himself through the eye of a minuscule tube, hoots going up from the beach behind me.

When the horn blows, I ride a wave in to shore on my stomach, hands folded over the tip of the board, then walk up the hard gleaming sand and sit in a daze facing the ocean, hugging my knees.

Carson squats beside me. "All right!"

I can't look at him. "Come on."

"What? You definitely took it!"

"What about Tommy?"

"He had one or two, but it's yours, dude."

We watch the eighth-grade finals. Sean Reilly, like Matt Thyme the son of a shaper, surfs as though he's a finger doodling fantasy turns in the sand: better and freer and faster than everyone.

Mr. Mash, the young science teacher who organized the contest, taps on a microphone. Carson and I rise and join the crowd around the judges' table.

There aren't many people present, but it's very nearly everyone in my world. Carla is there, it turns out, next to Mom on the boardwalk. Tyler is one of the judges. Though Meta seems to have left, which I take to be a bad sign.

"All right, people," Mash begins. He has a round, chubby face and wears braces. He's pulled a floppy canvas hat down hard on his head, but the skin of his hands is a fiery pink.

"People, we've seen some really fine competitive spirit out here today. Now, I don't surf myself—" There are scattered hoots at this.

Someone yells, "Mash on, Mash!"

"All right, Delgardo!" Mash says wearily. "We hear you.

"Now, as I say, I don't know much about surfing. But some excellent judges made truly tough decisions about winners and losers and they have kindly"—he waggles a clipboard—"given me the results.

"But before I announce the results of the contest, I want to thank Phil Meta and Darcy's Surf Shop for making this event possible." Scattered applause and hooting.

"Mr. Meta has informed me that the trophies are being custom-crafted and will be given to the winners at a later date."

Mash then reads the lists of the winners, beginning in seventh grade with third place and ascending quickly to ninth grade. As each name is announced, there are clapping and shouts of "Yeah!" and "All right!"

It's expected that I'll win. I've been surfing longest and I take it more seriously. In part because of that, there's a desire for Tommy to beat me. He's an ideal underdog—modest and small and smart. He gazes at the sand, hands crossed before his baggies.

"In second place," Mash says, "Tommy Stoltz." The cheers are perhaps undercut by a quiet moan of disappointment from his friends, but I can't be sure.

"And in first place, Thad Ziolkowski." I hear Mom's high voice hooting from the boardwalk. Adam runs down the beach to stand beside me.

Tommy walks over and we shake. "I knew you'd win," he says.

"Well, I didn't," I tell him. "Really. I thought you took it. Ask Carson."

On the way home, Adam says, "So does this mean you're the best in the whole school?"

"I guess."

"Sure it does," Pat says, looking at us in the rearview mirror. "He came in first in the ninth grade."

"Better," Adam says slyly, "than Sean Reilly?"

———

"Check it out."

The sea horse, ornate as a brooch and barely distinguishable from the sargasso weed I plucked it from, twines its tail around my little finger and lashes slowly back and forth.

Billy puts a hand up against the glare. "Wow," he says. "Where'd you find that?"

"Right here," I say, swirling the clump with my foot.

He holds out his hand and I pass it to him, droplets falling away like molten silver.

We're out at a no-name spot, Down South. I was checking the surf at Avenue B when he walked up beside me.

"Billy!" I found myself looking down at him. He is, it turns out, short.

"Hey," he said. "Wanna check it Down South? I have a car." We picked up Thatcher on the way.

When I asked about Kauai, Billy shrugged. "I got tired of waiting tables," he said. "But really I just got homesick, you know?"

No, I don't know. I thought when you left, especially for Hawaii, it was final.

"That's amazing." He passes the sea horse back to me. "You found that right here?"

"Yep." It troubles me slightly that he's so surprised.

I look at the sea horse then release it into the clear water between us. We watch it buck to and fro until it reaches the sargasso, entwines itself and disappears.

Mom looks up from the meat she's cutting for Jason and says, "Someone from Darcy's just called. Your trophy is ready."

I ride to Indialantic, drop my bike in front of Darcy's and go in. Meta looks up in disbelief. "That was fast!"

He looks older since being released, peaked, the flesh sagging on the bones of his face.

"Yeah!" I'm out of breath.

He shuffles through a stack of magazine-sized, bubble-wrapped squares, selects one and passes it across the laminated counter to me. I unstick the tape and peel away the bubble wrap.

The trophy is made of a half-inch layer of foam over which fiberglass and resin have been laid, like the deck of a surfboard.

"What do you think?" Meta asks.

It's as if the artist painted a portrait of my fantasy life: on a blue ground is an image in black of a surfer, one I recognize as based on a photo of Gerry Lopez banking off the top of a wave. Behind him is a half circle—the sun—and the track left by the board ends in a leaping dolphin.

In the lower right-hand corner is a small gold plate on which my name is inscribed, and "First Place Ninth Grade Hoover Junior High Surf Contest 1975."

I look up at Meta. He's speaking to someone on the phone now, his back to me.

"Oh my God, Phil, man, this is so—I don't even know—"

He glances back and flashes a distracted smile.

Seven

A nd life would simply go on like this forever, with now and then a slight descent perhaps, for the sake of humility, perspective, then upward again, nearer the sun, the islands of the Pacific. It's as if, with each wave I ride, I'm also ascending a single vast wave: the tradition of surfing itself.

And then everything changes.

"Pat lost his job yesterday," Mom tells me.

"You're kidding."

We're in the kitchen. She returns to chopping iceberg lettuce for salad.

"He never really got along with his boss—"

"God." I cast vaguely around the room as if for a better explanation.

"We'll work something out." She seems serene enough. "We have some ideas for how we can stay in Florida."

"We might have to move?"

"Not if we can help it."

Moving is not necessarily bad—to the contrary. The world in my mind, like some map out of Pliny the Elder or Saul Stein, is nearly all ocean and coast.

"We could move to Hawaii!"

She's weary of Hawaii. "Do you know what the cost of living is there? A head of lettuce is a dollar."

Pat comes into view on the lawn outside, stoops to fiddle with a sprinkler. He looks the same.

"Or California," I say.

"Now California is a possibility."

"But nowhere else."

She chuckles. "We'll do our best, honey."

I don't like the sound of that.

———————

Paddling against a slight north-to-south drift, I glance back at the beach to check my position and see Mr. Wheeler, the honors science teacher, cuffing up his trousers.

He walks down the sand and wades in, but there's a drop-off he doesn't seem to know about, and as he plunges to his waist he raises something overhead—a movie camera.

He trudges out of the trough and up onto the bar at the end of which Thatcher, Billy Olin's younger brother, and I are riding the shore break. The waves are on the small side but hollow, their tubes coughing up scarves of spray the offshore wind tosses stylishly over their shoulders.

When Wheeler sees me watching, he makes a helpless gesture indicating his drenched clothes, then gives a somehow over-eager thumbs-up. I wave.

He's tall and thin, chinless, Ichabod Crane neck, acne scars. I would feel sorry for him, only he seems to find my unstudious surfer posture a bit contemptible.

Yet here he is. He wants to gather data on surfing, I guess. I'll give him some data.

I scan for a wave. The last time I was filmed, I was eleven and on a secondhand twin fin. Under me now is a new purple swallowtail Meta gave me for free—well, almost for free.

I had been looking idly at it. Meta said, "You like?"

"Yeah. I need something shorter like this."

He was wearing corduroy walking shorts, Adidas tennis shoes and a Hawaiian shirt. His tan had returned.

"Do you really like it?"

"Well, yeah, Phil."

"Tell you what," he said, hopping backward onto the counter to sit erect, hands on knees, pharaonic. "Tell you what. Take the board home. I'll let you have it for cost—eighty bucks."

"Really?"

He smiled crookedly. "Yep."

"I don't have eighty bucks. I mean, I could get it, I guess—"

"So pay me when you get it."

"Damn, thanks, Phil!"

"You won't regret this!" I nearly added but thought better of it and simply stood there beaming until Meta bent slightly at the waist and made a rolling flourish with one hand, indicating the door and beach.

———

A set stands up. I whirl and take the first wave, noticing, out of the corner of my eye, Wheeler tracking the ride. It amounts to a quick turn and trim and ends abruptly when the wave closes out, though I duck into the tube at the last.

Two weeks later, he spots me in the river of students flowing through the hall and calls me over.

He's going to show the surf film to his afternoon classes—as "data on the local environment," he says with a wink. I knew it.

I leave another class early and lean with false casualness against the wall near the door of Wheeler's class. Beside me, one of the honors students, hand poised above the light switch, anxiously awaits Wheeler's signal.

The projector clatters, Wheeler nods, instantly the room goes dark and there it is again, the glassy blue ocean of that particular afternoon, its waves sending up spray as they pitch forward onto the shallow bar with inaudible concussions.

Now, viewed from a slightly southern angle, someone's paddling and with a jolt of both dread and pride I recognize myself.

Wheeler hoots and his students echo him as if responding chorally to a language instructor. I streak down the line away from the camera.

Something is awry, though. The new board looks too short. Or is it that my stance is wide and stiff? Instead of crouching in the tube, I squat and tip forward like someone trying to rinse his hair in a low sink.

Wheeler freeze-frames the film here and, knowing not what they do, the students hoot.

Hoping for redemption of some kind, some approximate match between my inner vision of myself and how I actually look surfing, I watch each wave impatiently, as if biting into a bad or tasteless piece of fruit then discarding it to try the next. On the better waves I seem to think the tube's at hand when it's behind me, and when it is at hand I don't slow down enough to get very far back inside it. I remind myself of a toddler who thinks he's disappeared from view because he's put his hands over his eyes.

Toward the end, Thatcher, two years my junior, paddles for a peak and rides well, gracefully, without effort, not surfing for the camera like me. The class perks up, instinctively appreciative. He's shown riding only a few waves but they're choice, and on the largest he crouches in the trough and lets the tube swallow him. For a few seconds only the speed-jittery tip of his board is visible. Wheeler pauses the film and everyone hoots again, a current of genuine enthusiasm running through it now.

As the lights come on, Wheeler claps his hands slowly, perhaps insincerely, at which the whole class applauds, their pale bespectacled faces turned toward me.

Maybe they think I'm Thatcher.

———

At the dinner table, Pat clears his throat. Adam and I tense up. If he's going to berate us for something, it's often here that it happens.

He tips his chair back and laces his fingers across his stomach. "What would you guys think of our opening a restaurant?"

"A restaurant?" I glance from him to Mom. She looks hopeful. "Cool."

"We have a spot picked out already. You know that marina in Indian Harbour?"

"Yeah. Matt Thyme's dad docked there for a while."

"We're thinking of calling it"—he forms an L-shaped frame with his hands—"the Ship's Inn.

"This would be sort of a family deal now. You guys will be waiters—well, Adam will start as a busboy."

I picture myself in black pants and a white shirt, saving tips for trips to Puerto Rico, Barbados, Eleuthera. The warmth of the kitchen, free food, beautiful waitresses.

"Sounds good," I say.

"Sounds great!" Adam says.

"Now, here's one of the things we're thinking about," Pat says, as if pitching the project to a backer. "It's what's called a 'salad bar.' Here's the deal: you set out your lettuce and tomatoes and croutons and what have you—bacon bits, a choice of salad dressings. Then the diners pay for a plate and make their own salads."

"Wow!" Adam says. "You make your own! Put in whatever you want!"

"Right," Pat says. "Pretty neat, huh?"

"When's all this going to happen?" I ask.

"Well, we have to get a loan from the bank first," he says offhandedly.

"A restaurant's a risky investment for a bank," Mom adds.

"But if we can get the loan," he replies, glancing at her, "and I don't see why we shouldn't, we should be open by late summer."

———

Buffed by an offshore breeze, the wave is prettier than it is powerful, but the new board skates across the flat spots. I wheel through a roundhouse cutback, sling a handful of soup behind me and squirt back down the line.

I'm the first out. It's like dancing in front of the mirror with the stereo turned up when no one's home. I wish Wheeler were here with his camera now. The new board, and having corrected certain things I noticed in the film, have improved everything, caused my surfing to leap forward.

Squaring up with the horizon for an off-the-lip, I'm briefly blinded by the sun, then turn a last time and, with a scissoring of my back foot, shoot the board across the lip and fall back to see it fly.

This one Meta did give me for free. He didn't say "Now you surf for Phil Meta Surfboards," oh but I do, I do.

The board sails through the air, lemon yellow against the blue sky, strikes the water on a rail and glides.

I dive, swim along the rippled bottom and surface to rest my chin and elbows on its deck. My hair is slicked back like a Jazz Age dandy's. I squirt an arc of water out between my teeth and squint into the refulgent glare.

When I look back at the beach, I see Dryden spreading the legs of his white tripod and for a tremendous moment believe he's come to photograph me at last.

But there's a surfer picking his way down the bluff. He jogs stiffly across the sand and into the shore break and soon reappears over the top of a wave, paddling with his chest arched high off the deck and hands dipped then drawn back as if in distaste. Just inside of the lineup, he scowls into the sun and wheels around to take a smallish wave. It's Jim Cartland, the surf star.

I know his sinewy, spring-loaded crouch from *Surfer*. Watching him now is like seeing these photos improvising themselves forward cinematically.

High in the pocket, he executes jittery turns, like a bird sifting the air for a vector of wind, dipping out of the trim to make a turn off the bottom then flashing back up to the pocket, then down again as if with reluctance, then up, then down, up, down, up, down, hummingbird-like, firing along faster and faster with each drop into the wave and finally, far down the beach (have the waves gotten longer?), kicking out.

As he returns to the lineup in front of Dryden, I smile shyly. Hi, Mr. Cartland, I'm a local dolphin!

Perhaps the sun is in his eyes.

As I did at eleven, Adam gets high, though in his case more often and with unadulterated relish, as if he's found his calling. How much Pat suspects is unclear until one day Adam's Little League coach appears alongside the fence where my team is warming up and beckons to Pat.

Pat is still coaching my teams, and I still pitch, though wildly. I think too much and throw well only when listening, as I am now, to the sonorous voice of the pitching coach. Pat calls my name and I trot over to him.

"Do you know where Adam is?"

"No."

"His game's starting and he hasn't shown up."

I shrug, uneasy now, and resentful: with Neal gone, Pat has been nicer, more human; Adam is rekindling the man's fire.

He bites his lower lip then signals to the pitching coach that we'll be back soon. "Let's go for a ride."

We cruise the breathless mid-afternoon streets. It seems

fairly hopeless. For Adam's sake, I hope it is. But Pat thinks like a detective. He slows at intersections, peers down streets, checks Avenue B, then parks in front of the 7-Eleven on Ocean Avenue and gets out.

Kids gather here in the evening. Now and then someone proffers a joint or a purloined bottle of Boone's Farm in a paper sack, but usually it's small-town wholesome: we drink Slurpees and brag, watch bats hunt. Once Neal and I regaled listeners with the story of the time Pat knocked a man down a hill for flirting with my mother at a party, our faces flushed with pride and bloodlust.

Now Pat's bending over the side of the very cinder-block wall where we sat telling the story about him. He seems to be feeling around for something; then, like a magician, an obstetrician, he jerks Adam up into the air by one arm.

Meanwhile, two kids break from cover at the far end of the wall, running in a crouch like routed soldiers.

Pat slaps Adam across the face, hauls him over to the car and tosses him in the backseat. No one speaks. Adam's shirtless—it's tucked into the pants of his uniform—and the side of his chest has been scraped by the cinder blocks.

I look at Pat. Blinking furiously, he grinds the stick shift into reverse. Sweat flings from the tip of his nose as he turns his head. It's the first time he's hurt either of us, even raised a hand.

Arms folded tightly across his chest, Adam blubbers quietly and seethes. He needs something to snap him out of his pot haze, but I doubt this will work, and Mom would be furious if she knew—not that I plan to tell her.

I watch part of his game. Adam seems half asleep in center field, but at bat, as if proving a point, he hits a pair of home runs.

I never once hit one.

Thad Ziolkowski

———

The tips of the Australian pines bow to the north in a side-shore breeze. There's no one on the beach or in the water with me, one of those endless afternoon moments in which I might be anyone or anything, a see-through sea god.

On a wave I do something, a sort of skidding slide along the top. After a while another wave lifts lumpily skyward and I put my head down like a cat and chase it. On my feet and rising to the crest, I think to try the slide again, think too much and fall.

The water stings as I strike it backward, but underneath it's warm as a whirlpool and I drift lazily downward, playing dead. I reach for the bottom with my feet, expecting to push off, encounter only more water and kick, the bubbles like time-lapse grapes forming at my lips.

I should have reached the surface by now. I open my eyes. It's a few feet away but something I can't see, a kind of invisible harness, is holding me under.

I flail my arms. It's a matter of inches now but I'm gagging. I gulp water. *I'm going to drown out here today, in three-foot surf.* It's as simple as not being able to get to the surface.

I have a vision of my corpse floating facedown in the shore break, as if the game Adam and I played had been rehearsal for this fate.

Released suddenly, I claw to the top and tear through it with an enormous gasp. I gag, cough up a bit of bile.

The foam on the surface fizzes blithely. There's not a wave in sight.

Ten yards away my board spins slowly, like the needle of a compass.

———

"Pat called earlier," Mom tells me.

It's evening. We're reading on the couch in the living room. No bank would loan money for the restaurant and he's been away on job interviews, the details of which I've shut my ears to, partly because he visits corporate headquarters in cities we won't have to move to even if he is hired, but mainly because I'm pretending that none of this is happening.

Flipping through the latest *Surfer,* I say, "Yeah?"

When there's no reply, I look up. She tucks a lock of hair behind an ear and purses her lips thoughtfully. She takes a sip of her tea, sets the cup down on the coffee table and curls her legs under her on the chair.

"He accepted a position with Boeing."

"He got a job?"

"A good one, too."

"We have to move, don't we?"

"I'm afraid so."

"Where?"

"Wichita."

My mouth falls open, I narrow my eyes. "Wichita, *Kansas?*"

She nods, her face as composed as an undertaker's.

I stare at her intently. "You're not kidding, are you?"

"No, honey, I'm not."

"That's unbelievable."

"I'm sorry."

"What about California?"

"We weren't given a choice among any state in the country."

"Okay, but Kansas?"

"Pat was lucky—"

I let out a whoop. "Lucky? You call this lucky?"

She raises a finger. "I will not discuss it with you if you can't talk calmly."

I stand up from the couch, the *Surfer* sliding to the floor. "Well, whatever," I say, shaking my head. "I'm not going."

As if waiting in ambush for this, she assumes her sternest tone, brow furrowed, finger leveled at me like a pistol. "You are not old enough to make that decision."

"What if I live with the Reynoldses?" Mrs. Reynolds has said that I would be welcome to live with them if we had to move somewhere awful. "My guys," she calls Carson and me, as if I've already been adopted. What the Colonel thinks about this prospect is another question.

Mom shakes her head decisively. "I'm not going to allow you to leave home this soon, Thad. You're too young. That's that."

I wave her off and stalk blindly down the hall to my room, pause at my door, then backtrack to the living room.

"But he grew up in Wichita!"

"That's true."

"How can he go back? It's not right!"

"That's just where the job is."

"Would you move back to Alabama?"

"If it were a question of making a living, of course I would."

"That's sick."

"You have to grow where you're planted."

"What? What's that supposed to mean?"

"Adapt."

Again I stalk to the door of my room then backtrack.

"Mom, look, I surf for Phil Meta."

"I realize that."

"It's, this is my life! I have a commitment to Phil! I'm like a professional! I've worked at this!"

"I know that," she says sympathetically. "You've seen us. We have tried every way we know to be able to stay in Florida, but it has simply not worked out."

I'm still shaking my head. "I can't believe this."

"I'm sorry."

"I can't fucking believe it."

"You're going to have to come to terms with it."

"We'll see about that," I tell her ominously. "We'll see about that."

Like someone diagnosed with a terminal disease, I sit for a time in shock, the surf posters on the walls of my room as mocking as cheery reproductions in the lobby of a cancer clinic.

Wichita, Kansas. Is there a drabber-sounding, more anti-surfing town in the country, in the world?

Adam and I used to play a game that consisted of speculating about the dullest places on earth, the sorrowful, bleak pastimes of people in, say, Scotland.

"Chess!" we would crow. "Flying *kites!*"

How could we have known that we were shuffling the cards of our future?

Eventually, I call Carson, who, as I assumed he would, invites me to live with him.

"I already tried that."

"And she said no?"

"Yeah. She sounded pretty definite."

"I'll have my mom call her. She'll talk her into it."

"It's worth a try."

"Hey, man, don't lose hope."

"Listen, I'll run away before I move to fucking *Kansas*. I will."

Carla drops by while I'm eating Sugar Smacks in the dining room. She stands next to the table and crosses her arms. "You're going to ruin your body with that stuff.

"Hey, what's wrong?"

I tell her.

She clutches my arm. "Thad, you won't survive there! Has your mother thought about that? Your skin, you'll, like, dry up and die, like a dolphin. Like Flipper in that episode where they take him on the plane and have to give him a sponge bath the entire way."

"Tell her that."

I ride my bike to Avenue B. Tyler's on the bench, one knee drawn up to his chest, stroking his dog's head as he gazes at unbreaking high-tide swells. When I tell him about Kansas, he glances at me then stares at the ocean.

"That's heavy," he says finally.

"Yeah."

"I personally don't know what to tell you, but I know Someone Who does."

"Oh," I say. "Okay."

I edge toward my bike.

Tyler turns to look directly at me now, eyes aswim with sincerity. "He's always there."

"Okay, Tyler," I tell him. "I better get back now."

Later that day, I run into Ed Hodge on Avenue B. Holding up one hand against the summer sunlight, he hears me out with his usual intensity, brown belly swelling like a wineskin as he breathes.

"Just come surfing," he says.

I nod slowly.

"Just . . . come . . . surfing," Hodge repeats, freighting each word. Then he turns and walks off.

I watch him go, stare at the pavement then pedal slowly through the streets. It's simple, isn't it? Kansas, the move—this whole crisis is nothing but a kind of trial. What's being demanded of me is that I give my life over to surfing, fully and without reservation. I have a vision of myself in Hawaii. They've moved away. I'm walking along the beach, pure, unalterable in my commitment. The sun shines on my shoulders.

A wooden plaque has been hung in the kitchen.

"God," it reads, "grant me the courage to change the things I can, the serenity to accept the things I can't, and the wisdom to know the difference."

Mom finds me standing before it.

"Yeah, well, I know the difference," I tell her darkly.

"I'm glad to hear it," she says.

We're enemies now, Queen Isabella and I. She is ordering me ashore.

I spot Meta leaning his elbows on the boardwalk railing. It's a gray, muggy afternoon, the waves minuscule and malformed.

I climb up onto the boardwalk and tell him the news.

"Wasn't there a restaurant in the works?"

"The loan didn't come through."

He shakes his head slowly. "Man, that's rough."

"It's worse than rough."

He stares at the ocean, then turns to me.

"This is going to sound like a crock to you, but in the long run? It might not be such a bad thing."

"What, moving to Kansas?"

"That's right."

If I didn't expect him to burst into tears or plead with my parents to allow me, for the sake of the future of surfing, to remain in Florida, I didn't expect this.

"There are other things in life besides surfing."

"Like *what,* for instance?"

"Like education—"

"I want to *just come surfing,*" I say, imitating Ed Hodge. "The school of *surfing,* Phil, you know?"

He puffs his cheeks with air and blows it out slowly, shakes his head.

"Go to the school of *school.* Go to college."

"College? I'm fifteen."

"Eventually, I mean. Isn't your dad a professor? Maybe you can go to college in California or Hawaii, where they at least," he raises his chin at the wind-battered wavelets, "have some real surf."

"Maybe," I say. "Later, someday. But fucking *Kansas,* Phil? How am I, what am I supposed to do in Kansas?"

"Read. Study for once in your life. I don't know. Get into running."

"Running?"

"Yeah, you look like you'd make a good four-forty man."

"How about running away?"

He looks at me under his brows. "Your folks would freak."

"My folks," I sneer.

"Listen, I have kids—I know. You don't want to cause them that kind of anguish. Not a good idea."

I stare at the surf and in a sad, physical sort of swoon, like falling ill, I realize there will be no running away.

"Not a good idea," Meta repeats.

I gaze hopelessly at the gray railing of the boardwalk, at the pitted sand of the beach.

"Look," he says, "when do you move?"

"October."

"Do you want to go out in style?"

"How?"

"The East Coast Championships in Hatteras. First week of September. You're qualified, right?"

"I think so."

"I'm driving the van up. Get registered."

Raking back his hair, Dryden lies down alongside the gutter and peers through the viewfinder of his camera. I can look directly at him now without my heart pounding unpleasantly. He bought our Volvo station wagon. Besides, what does it matter how well I know a surf photographer now?

It's late afternoon, the sky fading to lilac above the river behind us. Slim hips asway, Adam weaves down the street, hands poised just so, back foot folded onto the skateboard.

Dryden's doing an article on him for a new magazine devoted to skateboarding. I'm squatting on a lawn, observing the session in a state of mild disbelief. "Can I ask what you see in that?"

"Style!" he tells me, clicking the shutter. "Sty-le!"

"It's just a slightly stiff Jay Adams," I say, naming a skateboarder who's been appearing in *Surfer*. "And Adam's not banking off the coping of an empty pool like those guys."

"Do that thing with your feet!" Dryden calls as Adam passes by going the opposite way. "We're going to a ramp after this. You should see him on the ramp."

"I've seen him. I taught him most of this stuff."

Adam pushes off from the top of the street again, turns his feet so that the heels face each other and grips the ends of the skateboard with his toes, monkey-fashion.

"That's it!" Dryden says. Adam leaps balletically, bringing the board up and floating. Dryden clicks the shutter. "Great!"

"Oh, yeah," I say. "Amazing."

The Community Center on surf-movie night is like a windy sea—whitecaps of blond heads everywhere. The four of us have to split up, though eventually Corinne and I find seats together.

She and Dad have driven to Florida for the annual visit, in part a mission of mercy to spare us the trouble of going to D.C., though they've managed to find a local equivalent to the museums: Disney World. As if already looking back at it all, Adam and I have been giving them the tour—Sebastian Inlet, the boardwalk, Avenue B, Darcy's.

"So what's this one about?" Corinne asks.

Before I can explain, the lights go down, and from the crowd a low collective hoot rises.

Corinne leans over with a look of mild alarm. "What does this mean?"

"It's starting!" I shout above the din.

"You sound like monkeys!"

We do. Glancing around I see the scene through her eyes: the tans and hair, cheap foldout chairs, sand tracked across the bare floor.

As the first wave appears on-screen the hoots grow deafening. Corinne cups her hands to her mouth and joins in. Someone—it looks like Terry Fitzgerald—descends a vast green wall in slow motion, mop of hair abounce. Fitzgerald always looks as though he's riding through a wall of flames on a sword, an avenging barbarian.

"Santana!" Corinne shouts, identifying the soundtrack. I nod. She prides herself on knowing American music.

"*Abraxas?*"

I nod again but lean forward to discourage any more questions.

"I knew it!" she says. "I knew this!"

The drop alone takes a druggy eternity. When he disappears in the tube, the hooting reaches a crazed, rafter-swinging crescendo, then the crowd settles in for the rest, which consists, as always, of one wave after another.

Corinne turns to me with a puzzled, disappointed expression. "But there was no plot! It's just surfing!"

"That's right," I admit with a sigh. "It's just surfing."

———

Down South, I spy a pygmy rattler flowing through the palmettos at my feet. It's like encountering the totem of a dead religion. I point it out to Carson. We watch it vanish into the brush.

But if not snakes, and if not waves either, soon enough, what then? Autumn sweaters, sports, books?

Though distractedly, and always poised to jump ship if the surf came up, I've been playing football. I was named Defensive Player of the Year in ninth grade, albeit, I suspect, by default: the true star of the team had won all the other honors and the coach felt obliged to toss someone else a bone.

And there have always been, trickling over the sand, occasional rivulets of nostalgia for seasons and lamplight and mainstream glories. Can these be gathered into a single stream now, one I can drink from, find my reflection in?

———

The headlights of oncoming cars rake past Meta's shoulders and grainily sift the van's interior. Miller and Tyler doze on outspread sleeping bags, Dryden is loading a camera beside me and Ron

Thyme squats against the opposite wall like a Vietcong soldier. It begins to rain.

Riding shotgun is Dino, a chubby dark-haired crony of Meta's, the shady sort. He rummages in his duffel bag and places a square mirror on the raised molded plastic table and beverage tray between his seat and Meta's.

This is my first surf trip, it occurs to me, and my last: a self-canceling journey, leading to nothing, the foundation for nothing.

It's as if I do have a terminal disease and my surfing in the East Coast Championships has been sponsored by some charity as a kind of heartrending send-off, the equivalent of being allowed to throw a pitch in a Major League game before dying. No matter how well I do, even if I win my division, even if, at the awards ceremony, Greg Loehr himself bestows his trophy upon me in recognition of my having made history by outsurfing them all, this time next month I'll be in Wichita. Pat is there already, looking for a house.

From a small plastic bag, Dino pours onto the mirror a mound of what must be cocaine and commences chopping at it with a razor blade. Meta glances from the road to the mirror and back to the road.

Ron Thyme meets my eyes and smiles wryly, as if to say: some people never learn.

Having divided the cocaine into ruled lines, Dino turns toward the rear of the van and holds up a plastic drinking straw, like a conductor calling an orchestra to attention. No one takes up the offer.

He nods as if he expected as much and bends to inhale a line, sits back pressing the nostril closed with a finger, blinks thoughtfully, then bends to inhale a second line.

Dino reaches across and grips the steering wheel with one hand, peering through the rain-spattered windshield, the slosh of the wipers. Meta bends over the mirror, inhales three lines with swift expert swipes of the straw and sits up and takes the wheel back.

"Kansas," says Tyler. He's scooted along the floor to sit beside me. "Wow."

"I know," I say.

"But hey," he says softly. "He's there, too, you know? All you have to do is reach out."

Dryden, who appeared to be asleep, lifts his head. "Tyler, did it ever occur to you that some people may not want to reach out?"

Tyler shakes his head sadly. "No, Stan, not really."

"Well, give it some thought."

"What I mean, Stan," he says quietly, "is that people don't always know what they really want. They can't see it."

"But you can?"

Tyler purses his lips, an expression of resignation and apology to me for the presence of Satan/Stan. "So what's your answer, Stan?"

"My answer? A nice, secure job in a corporation. Forget about surfing."

"But Stan—"

"No, look around: a bunch of grown men with their knees up in the back of a van! We're like fucking migrant workers."

"Jesus was a migrant worker."

"Kansas is the best thing to ever happen to this kid and his brother. If they keep surfing they'll end up in some factory covered in foam dust."

I fall asleep, waking to the sight of Meta reaching over to steady the wheel, which is jerking to and fro under Dino's jittery hands.

We're crossing the long span bridge to the Outer Banks. It's still raining.

We check in to adjacent rooms in a motel near the Cape Hatteras lighthouse. Ron Thyme and I walk to the beach with our boards. The land here seems a mere spit of sand, scrub brush, mosquitoes. Gray sky, gray waves. He points out the "groins," low iron fences that jut into the surf every seventy-five yards or so to prevent erosion.

Thyme is having trouble catching waves. His muscles still look as though they were stamped in bronze, but he has a bad back. He sits like a decoy of a surfer in the dusk, the rain falling harder.

As I paddle back out after a wave, he says, "If you surf like that in the contest, you'll win it."

"You think?"

He nods. "Without a doubt."

And what if I did win? It won't change Mom's mind—nothing will—but it would make her feel guiltier for uprooting me. That will have to do.

The next morning, the air and water are pearly and wind-blown, as in open ocean, and the waves are over six feet, longer and thicker than any I've seen. My thighs ache at the end of a ride, as from skiing. The unsmiling crowd swells with the arrival of contestants. By mid-morning, to claim a set wave I have to position myself behind its peak, which invariably forms at the head of one of the groins.

Three of us are paddling. Through the spray I can make out foam boiling around the gnarled, rust-encrusted iron as the water is drawn back in cords.

I jump to my feet and make the drop, but at the bottom the plate skitters then spins out and I'm swept across the groin. I clutch my own groin with both hands, surface unscathed, swim in, pick up my board in the shallows and walk up the beach.

I find Meta in the parking lot and ask to borrow the 6'8" spear he brought along in case the waves got big. He gestures at the van's rack.

When I get the board down, Meta calls, "Your heat's scheduled for three. Think you can get this board wired in time?"

Before I can answer, he turns to lead a blonde back toward the motel, the first in a procession.

I sit on the beach beside Dryden and his tripod and camera. Though smaller, the waves remain long and thick. The first heat of the Men's Division is about to be announced.

Dryden says, "I don't necessarily believe everything I said in the van. I just react badly when Tyler gets all Jesus Freaky."

He doodles in the sand. "I have a family to worry about and there I am busting my ass sanding boards all day? I have no retirement plan, nothing."

He smooths the sand and peers through his viewfinder. "It just bums me out to see smart kids like you and your brother headed down the same road."

A flock of sandpipers flares open before us then swings toward the waves, veers back to shore and lights on the gleaming sand.

"So why do you keep taking photos and stuff if surfing's such a bad idea?"

"It's beautiful," he blurts. Then, as if to erase this, he adds, "And it pays, don't forget. A little."

At noon, I buy subs from a stand set up in the parking lot.

When I pass one to Dryden, he points with it at the surf. "There's your competition."

I shield my eyes. "Which one?"

"Wait, here comes a set. You'll see."

Finally, at the edge of the contest area, a small wiry kid hops to his feet at the peak of a thick wave. In the time it would take me to set up my first turn, he slashes two S's from a low rubbery crouch, tapping the water with his hands as if reassuring it. The wave doubles up nastily and as the bottom drops out he flicks up into the pocket and calmly disappears into its swollen throat like a child sacrifice.

"Damn."

"Cody something, from Virginia Beach."

"Virginia Beach? Do they even get waves there?"

"Evidently."

At four o'clock, the first heat of the Boys' Division is announced over the PA system. The sky has cleared and the waves are glassy, small enough for the plate. There will be no excuses. My limbs feel hollow.

"Tad . . . ?" the announcer asks. There's a helpless pause. "Zee-ow?"

"That must be me," I tell Thyme gloomily.

"So, surf so good they'll remember how to say it right."

I walk through the crowd to the judges' table.

"Zye-low?" the announcer asks. "Tad?"

"I'm Ziolkowski," I tell him.

Two of the contestants are staring at me as if having grave doubts about my eligibility for the Boys' Division. Technically, I'm not eligible: I turned fifteen months ago. Meta got around it somehow.

I'm tossed a blue jersey. Cody from Virginia Beach, an impish, carefree smile at play on his lips, is wearing red. I force myself to look away from him.

Meta motions for me. I trot over to him.

"Sit outside and wait for the sets," he tells me in a low voice. We're both looking at the surf. "Don't get distracted by the smaller stuff."

I nod.

"But remember now, only the first two places advance to the finals."

The air horn sounds. I rejoin the others and we jog into the shallows, leap onto our boards and paddle. I'm the only one without a surf leash.

I paddle farthest out and sit up. Swells ripple past the corrugated iron of the groin; the sound of Cody's spray raining down on the backs of smaller waves reaches my ears.

Five minutes pass without a set. I look back at the judges' table, the massive barber-pole lighthouse, the sun behind it.

It's now been ten minutes. Have I taken Meta's instructions too literally?

Cursing softly, I chase down a small wave. When I try an off-the-lip, my back foot slips. I lunge to hug the board and it strikes my chin with a crack. I catch another small wave and manage to link a series of turns.

When I kick out, a set is coming. The waves are like moving folds of green silk. It's like the arrival of a new spirit, an awakening. The air is infused with hope and energy.

Cody takes the first, the boy in yellow the second. The last is the biggest, its ice-blue lip already hurling forward and out with a sound like "Cow!"

It's the wave of the heat, of the day perhaps. I spin and catch it without a stroke. My mouth opens as the board drops away, my arms lift above my head like wings and my legs extend until my feet are on point, only the toes touching the deck. Then, recovering, I turn off the bottom and float up into the pocket.

I'm grinning now, passing through panels of sunlight, the eyes of the crowd upon me, as if I'm running a victory lap.

––––––––

I place third, failing to advance. I receive the news numbly. Ron Thyme smiles as if to show me how, shrugs. I wring out the blue jersey.

I've never lost a surf contest before. It seems part of the larger sweep of bad luck overtaking my life. Worse, perhaps I'm simply not what I thought I was—gifted; perhaps I won before because the competition was feeble.

That night, I remove the Gideon's Bible from the drawer of my bedside table and open it at random. Meta and the rest are out at a bar—all except Tyler, who advanced to the finals of the Seniors' Division and has gone to bed early.

I sit up straight on the edge of the bed and read with a chastened, humble demeanor, the way I sometimes gravely opened a textbook on the first evening after school began, in a kind of trance of good conduct. I imagine myself at a turning point, an altogether different future, one of beatific selflessness, opening before me.

The thin page gleams in the lamplight, but the text itself is impenetrable. Hoping for a visitation of some sort, a light, I read on. Nothing happens. Finally, Dryden enters the adjoining room with a clatter and I hastily return the book to its drawer.

The finals of the Boys' Division are held late in the afternoon on the next day, the last event of the contest. Many people have already left.

I watch from the beach. Meta's van is idling in the parking lot, boards stacked on the roof. The surf has dropped to the point where it's nearly flat.

"They should call this off," Ron Thyme remarks beside me.

"Truly," I agree, but secretly find it perversely consoling. Cody's quick turns seem panicky, as if he's surfing on willpower alone.

A seemingly endless lull sets in, the ocean like a mind trailing off into final thoughtlessness, merging with sky.

It's as if surfing is dying.

Eight

In the seat beside me on the plane, Adam reads yet again Dryden's article in *Skateboarder Magazine,* muttering the words like a prayer: "A popular misconception about skateboarding, at least in Florida, is that the really hot skateboarders are in the 14-and-older age group. But at age eleven, Adam puts down all these beliefs."

Mom and Jason are asleep. I squeeze past them and trudge through the cabin. On top of everything else, my face has broken out. I want to assess the damage in the bathroom.

The muffled roar of the jet and thin, wintry sunlight lend the trip along the aisle a weightless, dream-like quality. I also seem to be passing into a previous era: the women have primped Doris Day hair, the men wear penny loafers, oxford shirts.

The plane plummets briefly, and as I reach out to steady myself against an overhead compartment, a man with a brush cut and pale waxy skin looks up from an in-flight magazine. My own hair falls to my shoulders. He's wearing a green crew-neck wool sweater, a college ring. His expression is profoundly sober.

Now what, he seems to wonder, is this boy supposed to be?

The boy wonders the same thing.

Back in my seat, I open *Something Happened,* a Joseph Heller novel I found among Mom's books. But several chapters in, I decide that it's the bleakest thing I've ever read and snap it shut in a panic.

The noise wakes Adam. He peers around sleepily and leans across me to look out the window.

It's a clear night, thirty-seven degrees, according to the captain. Below us, merciless in its actuality, Wichita glitters.

The landing gear rumbles like a knell.

———

We stay the first night at a Holiday Inn. Pat is quiet and hesitant, as if ashamed of where his life has led us. I can bring myself neither to reassure nor, finally, to blame him. The scale of this exile is too vast to be someone's fault.

In the morning, walking to the car, Mom points. "Look."

I think she means to draw my attention to the blue Kansan sky, the mare's-tail clouds. But it's the signboard in front of the hotel, the movable black letters of which read, "Welcome: Pat Burke and Family."

For a moment I actually feel honored, then the sadness of it sinks in—a sign on a Holiday Inn in Wichita—and I'm more depressed than ever.

When I open the car door, a gust of wind snatches it from my hand and nearly buckles the hinges. The main streets at the east end of town are laid out at right angles, lined with Burger Kings and Pizza Huts, Hardee's and Dairy Queens. At the center of it all, like an evolutionary leap or apotheosis, is a white shopping mall stretching for acres.

The house Pat bought is in an older neighborhood with winding streets, shaggy oak and elm trees, broad shapeless hedges separating the lawns. The rooms reek of cat piss, but for that reason it came cheap. I clean all morning alongside Mom and Pat; then, after lunch, he tosses me the car keys.

"Why don't you head over to the Y and sign up? Check out the weight room."

He wants me to go out for the high school football team. So do I. What else is there here?

He draws a map of the streets with his gold Cross pen.

It's the middle of a school day and no one else is there. I lift for an hour then go to the showers, thinking back to the first school days in Florida, the sea turtle, the first surfer.

As if to rub my nose in the difference between there and here, a man appears beneath a shower across the stall, lathering his chest and crotch again and again and peeking at me through the spray.

Waiting for the school bus, I touch my wet hair. It's frozen in two sheets on either side of the part. I feel an urge to snap them off like the wings of a cicada.

Southeast High is a sprawling tan brick building, three or four times the size of the one in Melbourne. Their hair arranged in complicated lacquered wings, the most striking girls seem to aspire to Farrah Fawcett, while many of the boys comb their bangs forward in a Beatles cut. They wear plaid shirts and sleeveless down jackets. A few turn to appraise me.

I'm not who I am, I tell myself. I'm someone mysterious and menacing, a blend of Clint Eastwood and Jimi Hendrix. I walk with a bounce in my left step. In biology class, a girl asks me where I'm from and I reply as if from a remote, stoned planet. She mocks the slurry way I speak and then ignores me.

At noon, I go to the cafeteria. It's nearly empty. Most of the students drive cars and leave campus for lunch. In line, a black kid steps in front of me and another, behind me, shoves him on the shoulder.

"Niggah, that ain't right!"

The kid shoots us both a glare.

"Don't mind that triflin' motherfucker."

I shrug. "It's all right."

He clucks his tongue. "No, it ain't.

"So where you from with your suntan?"

"I still have one?"

He has green eyes, freckles on his cheekbones. "Compared to the white folks around here, you're as black as I am."

"Florida."

His eyes light up. "Palm trees, nice warm water."

"Right."

"Nothing like that here, my man."

"Nope."

"And you don't look too happy about that."

"I'm all right."

"But just all right."

"Right."

The final class of the day is canceled for a pep rally. In Melbourne, where the team was mediocre, the band played off-key renditions of songs like the "Theme from Shaft." Over feedback from the microphone, the principal usually said a few words about poor attendance; the coach shouted a quick prayer for victory or reproached us for our lack of spirit; and a handful of cheerleaders cartwheeled across the creaky wood floor.

Here the team has won four consecutive state championships. So far this year they are undefeated. The games are broadcast on the local radio, covered on the front page of the city newspaper. I already know the name of the legendary coach—Huff.

The rally is held in the large, ornate auditorium. There are hundreds of plush seats and every one of them is taken. Students stand in the aisles, along the back wall. Banners hang from the stage and crepe in the school colors is swagged from the walls. The band is crisp, the cheerleaders and pom-pom girls nubile. One after the other, the team captains walk out onto the stage and say a few heartfelt words about the upcoming game against the city rival. The assistant coaches follow. The cheering grows louder. When Coach Huff himself is finally announced and swaggers out to grab the microphone, the roar is like something for Mick Jagger or Mussolini—so overwhelming that I can't make out what he's barking. The walls are vibrating. He's making uppercuts at the air with his fist.

———

We go as a family to the house of a coworker of Pat's from Boeing. In Florida, Pat marketed laser technology. Here, it's a device police stations can use to track patrol cars. No wonder he sounds bored discussing it.

After dinner, the teenage daughter, Marcy, takes me out in her car. We stop a few blocks away to pick up a girlfriend. She's stunning. The night sky is enormous and indigo, drilled open by stars. I sit between them in the fragrant cloud rising from their hair, jean-clad thighs, the breasts beneath their ribbed sweaters. We drive fast along ruler-straight roads, fields and glowing silos, then turn down a dirt road and stop.

Are we about to have sex, the three of us? Maybe that's how things are done in Kansas.

The girlfriend slips a joint from behind her ear.

"Wanna smoke a doobie?"

"Oh. No, thanks."

They look at me, then each other, then back at me.

"How come?"

"Yeah, we thought you were cool."

"I am—cool. I just don't smoke anymore."

The girlfriend narrows her eyes. "Anymore? Have you even smoked it before?"

"Sure, I'm just not into it now."

A silence falls over the car.

Marcy says, "How can you not be into pot?"

"Yeah, come on, one joint."

"No thanks, but you guys go ahead."

They look at each other across me again. The girlfriend strikes a match and lights the joint. The aroma fills the car. "Look, it's just pot!"

"Yeah, it won't kill you!"

Suddenly she's pressing the joint to my lips. "Take a hit, one hit—to prove to us that you're cool!"

I have to grab her by the wrist and pry her hand away. It's like a scene from an educational film about drugs and peer pressure, only more laughably unrealistic. And I would laugh except it's arousing, this attempt at big-sister intimidation.

And it's too late for the truth: the circle of us under the tree, my eleven-year-old heart pounding, Billy grinning as I rode that first wave in the moonlight. Like a rocket stage, all that has fallen unprovable worlds away.

———

After school, I go to the Y, the stack of plates on the Universal machine rising and falling behind my head with a creak. I shall build myself into a massive, invincible linebacker. At 6'2" I'm tall enough already. All I need to add is sixty pounds of muscle.

Other than a lone basketball player, high school age, there's no one else here at this hour. I watch him run the floor. We're like inmates released from solitary for exercise. He has straight blond hair, the bland good looks of a cowboy and a flawless, balletic jump shot.

He begins trying to dunk, charging the rim over and over, cursing himself. Finally, two days later, the ball flashes through the hoop.

He wheels around. "Did you see that?" Until now he's ignored me.

"Yeah!"

"I can jam!" As if to be certain, he dunks twice more then slams the ball off the floor and introduces himself.

"Donny." He turns to look back at the court in a way that reminds me of how I glanced back at the ocean from the beach. "Man, I can't believe I can jam now!"

"So what team do you play for?"

"I go to Southeast," he says, face clouding.

"You're not on the team?"

He shakes his head. He had a falling-out with the coach, he tells me later. He's like an artist—touchy, perfectionistic. He lives nearby in a small house with his mother, a secretary, and practices alone most of the day, playing pickup games at night, slowly flunking out of school.

Now Adam appears with his skateboard—the polyurethane wheels work well on the court—glances over at us to be sure we've noticed and begins a series of flashy tricks.

Donny's jaw drops. "Are you watching this?"

"That's my brother. I've seen it all before."

"Damn, where'd he learn that?"

I take a breath and begin telling him about the heaven from which we fell.

———

Otherwise, it's books I plunge into. I read Hesse, Hemingway, Thomas Wolfe, Michener, whatever comes to hand, many of them given to me by Mom. I read as I walk to the bus stop, on the bus, I read during classes. I read to drown myself.

Algebra is taught by a credulous elderly woman. I already know the terms—variables, coefficients, polynomials. I have no idea how to solve problems, but since she thinks I'm ahead of the curve, I write letters to Carson, and to Carla, describing Kansas for them, the cars and fashion, the howling wind, the strangeness. Then I begin cutting class altogether.

I vow to learn so much on my own that failing will redound to my credit. It's wisdom I crave, the consolation of philosophy.

I read Plato, Freud, opening classics at random, becoming lost, losing interest.

Andre is the name of the student from the cafeteria. I spend time with him in the section of school claimed by the black students, their lockers side by side for long stretches of hallway.

"Show us your walk," he says one day.

"I don't have a 'walk.'"

He waves me off and does an imitation. It's Billy Olin's strut, surviving, unbeknownst to me, in my body all these years.

Parliament Funkadelic thumps out of chest-high speakers. A Soul Train line forms, people crowd around it. One or two are not happy to see a white boy here, but most don't mind, and a few smile. The boys wear high-waisted pants, platform shoes and Quiana shirts unbuttoned to the breastbone. Their hair is pomaded. They look like pimps.

> *If you hear any noise,*
> *It's just me and the boys,*
> *Hit me.*

Shuffling sideways and clapping to the beat, the people in the Soul Train line dance between the facing rows to the far end. A boy with hair brushed back like Frederick Douglass slides his platform shoes across the floor, mysteriously, as if on invisible ice. A girl appears behind him, flowing in and out of view, face blank. He does the splits, springs back up, spins, swirls his coat in a slow veronica above his head.

It's the closest thing to surfing I'll see here.

––––––––––

It's been two months and still I'm like someone marooned on a planet whose atmosphere might not be safe. Socials, Freaks, Greasers, Jocks—the school is a collection of well-defined social groups, but I fit easily into none. Andre and the black students offer a kind of welcome, but I'm not black, either.

Rain blows at a hard slant against the school's safety-mesh windows. In gym, an assistant football coach herds us into a small, hot room for wrestling. Daily weight lifting has thickened my muscles dramatically and he wants to see me wrestle but can find no match for me among the others.

Students make nonchalant suggestions. "How about Keith?"

"Too fat."

"What about Brian?"

"Not enough muscle."

Finally he crooks a finger at a tall black student he passed over originally. "Come on, Russ."

The class falls silent, crowds around us. The black kid gets down on all fours. I kneel, clasp one hand around his wrist, sling an arm around his chest.

As in other classes, barely a word has been said to me. The entire school seems to have known each other since kindergarten. I'm the equivalent of a tourist at the boardwalk—unreal, a ghost.

So it's shocking when, at the whistle, they bellow, "*Get 'im, Russell!*"

"*Beat this kid!*"

"*Kick his ass, Russ!*"

"*Kick this kid's ass!*"

It's deafening. They're hopping up and down on the edge of the mat like baboons.

"*Flip 'im over, Russ, flip 'im over!*"

Their ferocity and hatred make me want to give in, to give them what they want, and I wrestle distractedly until the coach calls it a draw.

———

At the beginning of the spring semester, thinking to impress my father, but also simply thinking about him, I enroll in a Latin class. It's time I started attending courses that might get me into college. At the university where he teaches, tuition is waived for children of faculty, but there's more glory in returning to Florida on a football scholarship and I've decided in favor of that future. I spoke to Coach Huff about it when he approached me in gym class. I'd been pointed out to him by other coaches because of my size. "I'll see what I can do for you," he said. It was like making initial arrangements with a mafioso.

Meanwhile, because it reminds me of my father, studying Latin is pleasurable in a sad way, like reading epitaphs. I have strange, nostalgic intuitions of things I associate with him— northeastern autumns, duty, scholarship, self-abnegation. It's as though he's entangled in the syllables, lodged in the diphthong ae; as if by learning these things I'm also invoking him.

As long as we study vocabulary I do fine. But now it's time to parse sentences. Strange, I don't seem to know the first thing about the parts of speech. Embarrassed, but lazy too, I decide to drop the course.

I prepare a parting speech.

"It must not be genetic," I tell the dry, skeptical instructor, "because my father teaches Latin in college."

"Is that so?" she says, unimpressed or disbelieving, and signs the drop slip.

———

In a down-at-the-heels shopping center, many of whose storefronts are unrented, Mom and Pat open a skateboard store. It's a sideline to the Boeing job, but also a plausible business venture: skateboarding is suddenly popular nationwide. Adam and the shop are featured in the newspaper. Copies of this and Dryden's *Skateboarder Magazine* article are handed out to customers.

Like a live advertisement, an evangelist, Adam rides on the mall's broad empty walkway, passing one way in a handstand, back the other doing a wheelie, pausing to begin an endless series of three-sixties, hands clasped prayerfully. Suddenly he's an asset to the family, a kind of authority and child star. In matters of what sort of equipment to order for the shop, Pat defers to him.

But they remain at odds. If anything, Adam smokes even more pot than he did before the 7-Eleven incident; several times

Pat has just missed catching him, stalking around the corner of the house on a hunch as Adam flicks the last of a joint into a hedge and glances up with a guilty start.

I help out at the shop, assembling trucks and wheels at the workbench behind the front counter, making change at the old-fashioned register. But only when I'm asked to.

I brought nothing with me, no *Surfers*, no baggies, not a crumb of wax. Well, I didn't stop Mom from packing the trophies. But I'm doing my best to forget about surfing, and what is skateboarding if not a default version—surfing stripped of the ocean and its magic, like a taxidermic dolphin? Yet I'm unable to stop talking about Florida. It's my Jerusalem, all I have to make sense of my wandering in this desert.

———

Pat buys a second car, a used white Oldsmobile convertible, and lets me drive it to school. Passing through the dark town, I arrive before classes to lift weights with the football team. The star seniors, huge blonds and blacks on their way to scholarships at the state colleges, smile upon me as retiring soldiers upon a promising recruit. Their parties are spartan: a keg and bonfire alongside a remote farm road. I drink beer from plastic cups and gaze at the faces of cheerleaders in the light of the flames.

I drive to the skateboard store to have lunch with Mom. It's mid-winter, the huge trees dark with melted snow, shorn. She's given me her battered cloth edition of *You Can't Go Home Again*, inscribed with a dedication about the importance of the book in her own life when she was sixteen. I open it on the glass counter between us and read aloud a passage that impresses me. Her life, I see, has always been conducted here—not in books, exactly, but in the air. Which is why it never really mattered to her where we lived.

Later, flipping through a file of index cards for the name of a supplier, she seems wistful, resigned. Perhaps Kansas is proving bleak for her too. Things are not the same in her marriage here, though exactly how is hazy, probably because I don't want to see; that something retain its former appearance is more important.

———

Encouraged by the track coaches, I give the javelin a try. It wobbles a woefully short distance through the spring air, the prairie light I'm beginning to appreciate, strikes the moist sod on point and slowly tips over. Fortunately, not many people are watching.

Pat strolls up in the dark blue windbreaker he wore coaching my teams in Florida. I'm glad to see him.

"How'd you do?"

"Someone has to come in last."

He chuckles.

We lean on the fence and watch the distance runners. It occurs to me that the meet is being held at East, his high school.

"Do you remember your old school?"

Mom recently brought out a shoe box stuffed with drab black-and-white photographs: a baby-faced Pat grinning in the middle row of high school teams—wrestling, baseball, basketball.

He gazes at the buildings.

"Sure," he says. "You never forget."

"You were Big Man on Campus here, weren't you?" A Bad Boy Most Likely to Succeed type, Mom said. It's not hard to picture.

"Yeah," he mutters, face darkening. "So what the hell am I doing back here?"

In July, I visit Carson in Los Angeles, where surf culture has been carried to one conclusion: anorexic beach bunnies in micro bikinis, waves ridden under Huntington Pier floodlights at midnight. Watching it, I feel a mild tug of nostalgia, a sociological curiosity. I weigh well over two hundred pounds, my muscles round and smooth like those of a Samoan bouncer, like a body grown in a vat. My hair is cropped short. I'm a football player now.

Or am I? I'm riding the team bus to the first game of the season in early September. The pale stadium looms, yet I'm unmoved. What do I really care about beating this team, any team? I'd rather read about it. I feel, curiously, that I am reading—or writing a letter to Carson about it.

Those bastards! I tell myself. I need to get angry. *They've— what have they done? They've raped your mother!*

But I don't believe it, and the game seems played underwater, as slow as a dream, as frustrating. I lumber after the halfbacks, the quickness that was my only natural gift smothered beneath the methodically acquired pounds. It feels as though I'm wearing four wet suits. Why didn't I notice this in practice? The coaches must have: that's why I'm in the middle of the defensive line, being hit from four or five directions at once, as in a car crash at an intersection.

Not only do we lose, but the next day I have knots on my head, ominously sore knees. Why do this to myself?

But no one quits this team. When they learn of my decision, the captains, polite A-student types, spend an afternoon in my kitchen, like social workers, or police attempting to talk someone away from a building ledge.

Finally, I knock on the door of Coach Huff's office.

"It's open!" He sits hunched over his desk, his rugged brow furrowed, twisting a paper clip. Passing down the hall outside the office windows, players rubberneck.

The last time I saw him, the team was morosely watching the game film. "You *stood him up*, Ziolkowski!" he shouted at the screen when I finally got involved in a play. Shuffling sideways in the arms of the offensive lineman, I looked like a bear on its hind legs. "Now *stop dancing with him!*" He rewound the sequence and ran it forward again in slow motion. "Get *rid* of him," he turned to bark at me, "*get rid of him, get rid of him!*"

"Look, it's your decision," he tells me now. "I think you should come out to practice this week and see how it feels, but I'm not going to plead here."

"Well," I say. "I don't know, I just can't get into the violence of football anymore."

Huff rolls his eyes.

"Fine," he says tightly. "But you'll have to turn in your game-day shirt."

———

Carson, when we speak on the phone, says, "So move back! What's to stop you now? Finish school here."

"Yeah, I guess I could ask again."

"You could study with Exley." Exley is a therapist and former radical priest who's set up an alternative-to-suspension program within Melbourne High. Carson's been rhapsodizing about him.

"Also," he adds, lowering his voice, "Mom and the Colonel are probably getting a divorce. So he won't be around much longer."

"That's good."

But do I want to go back? I finally have a girlfriend, a studious blonde with whom I park on weekend nights in a spot I find by a sort of sexual homing instinct, the Oldsmobile windows slowly steaming up. As the autumn days shorten, I read, write. I'm content; it's as if I'm in the dark of some womb, undetected by the sun gods who once knew my name and monitored my daily devotions to the waves.

Sensing my ambivalence, Carson and Carla call to make their case. "Come home," they say. "You belong back here."

I find Mom folding clothes in the basement. She's sitting in Pat's easy chair.

"Carson and his mom said that, if you agreed, I could live at their house. You know, finish high school down there begin-ning next semester, in January." It's October.

She smooths one of Jason's tiny shirts. There's a Ping-Pong table in the corner, scattered toys, a shelf of trophies. The "family room," it's called. And there are nights when, in the fog of the TV light, a sort of sleepy unity does settle over us.

"Is that what you want?"

I'm not sure, but I shrug, nod. "I'm not playing football. There's nothing to keep me here now."

A wounded expression flickers across her face, to be replaced by one of slightly sour judiciousness. For an instant it's as on the afternoon she broke the news about the move to Kansas. Only we're no longer Queen Isabella and Columbus. The terms have changed, like the landscape outside the window, though into what I'm not sure.

"Well," she says. "You'll be seventeen in a few months." She folds another shirt, regards me solemnly. "I believe you're mature enough to leave home to finish school now, if that's what you want."

"I think so too."

"I guess you could go in January," she concludes.

"Thank you," I say. "That's great."

But in the weeks to come, I wonder. How, now that it barely matters, I'm free to go.

———

I knock on Adam's door. "Just a minute," he calls over the Jimi Hendrix. "Who is it?" His voice has deepened with the onset of puberty.

"Me."

I hear "It's my brother."

A long moment passes, then the door opens. Adam's face wears a look of complex abashment. He's stoned.

Behind him, waving his arm by an open window to clear the smoke, is a crippled boy, his aluminum crutches crossed on the carpet. Adam's friends are drawn from among the wounded now, outcasts of one sort or another. It's one of the ways in which he's changed in the past year, grown stranger, the breathless boy being replaced by someone who stands at a distance and is often displeased by what he sees.

"Man, you better be careful with that," I warn, lifting my chin toward the window. "Take it outside."

"It's cool," he says. "They went out to dinner."

"Two hours ago. Where's Jason?"

His eyes widen. "He's not with you?" He grins, and opens the door wider to reveal Jason kneeling over a coloring book on the floor, his head bobbing to the beat of the music.

"Oh, great."

Adam snickers, gazes at his feet; then, remembering suddenly, looks up and says, "You leave tomorrow, don't you?"

"Yeah, before you get up. I thought I should, you know—"

"Damn, I can't believe it."

"Me neither, really."

"Well, tell everyone 'hi' for me. You know, Dryden, Tyler, Carson. Tell them I'll be down this summer."

"All right, man." Awkwardly, I draw him to me. "Look after Mom for me, take care of Jason."

He rests his face in the hollow of my shoulder then withdraws, eyes fixed on the floor.

I cross the room and kneel to hug Jason. He's a little boy now, with large blue eyes and long lashes, a boy out of *Grimm's Fairy Tales.*

Pat drives me to the airport before dawn. I said good-bye to Mom late last night, though we had said good-bye weeks earlier, and it was the merest gesture. We pass the Holiday Inn with the sign that once read "Welcome: Pat Burke and Family," and continue out along the same road we drove in on. Snow sifts across it like phosphorescent sand.

Little is said, but at the same time I feel closer to him than I ever have, as if my departure were a door opening to release the warmth that had built up behind it.

He looks much as he did seven years ago, when we met—hair thinner, perhaps, but still jet black; the somewhat jowly cheeks, handsome nose, serious, preoccupied gaze.

He's as unreasonable as ever: in August, when someone plowed into the Oldsmobile while I was at the wheel, he flew into a rage. I was devastated. "It wasn't my fault! It was an accident!"

"There's no such thing as an accident!" he shouted.

But I'm not brooding about that now. It's essentially over, our struggle. Yet the feeling in the car is more than that of a truce, more even than companionable silence.

Unexpectedly, it's closer to love.

Nine

I peer into the cold water, my feet bone-white below the hem of black neoprene, then out at the capillary-like streaks of surface current. Has it noted my absence?

An ellipsis of foam appears onshore, catches the winter sunlight, withdraws like a tongue. It doesn't say, though, as often, the feeling is that it might.

Everyone's hair is longer. Thatcher has been smoking so much pot that his face, like that of an alcoholic, is marked by it, Toby too. I'm welcomed back without much comment, as if emerging after a convalescence or prison term.

Carson has a feathery mustache and a girlfriend, vulgar but voluptuous, disapproved of by Mrs. Reynolds. Their song is "The Way We Were," an eight-track of which they play in the car stereo on the way to and from school. On weekend nights, they and friends unfamiliar to me set up tents on the beach and fish for sharks, an enthusiasm I don't understand. It's like hauling a piano to shore; lying on the sand, the sharks appear worse than inert—shorn of mystery, profaned.

On my first day back to school, Carson arranges for me to miss my final class and ushers me into the presence of Tim Exley, the teacher/therapist he has spoken so highly of.

Exley has a deep tan, hooded gnome-like eyes, an aquiline nose, well-trimmed beard the brown of his thinning hair. We've just watched him beat a group of students in volleyball, three games in a row. He bet his heavy silver Rolex watch. It was a demonstration of Satyagraha, a Gandhian term that he refuses to define. He moves wizard-like in a cloud of such terms—"the power of the group," "phenomenology," "thinking 'outside the lines.'"

Now he's stuffing books into a briefcase. Head cocked, I'm idly trying to read the titles. The scuffle of students passing along the open-air hallways is audible through the door and the louvered windows through which sunlight passes.

"So what are you up to now, Tim?" Carson asks. He's different with Exley, his speech breathless and coded. I'm trying not to let it annoy me.

Exley looks up from his books and beams with child-like enthusiasm. "I have a project!" He has a lilting southern accent. He grew up in Georgia, Carson told me, and went to Emory.

"What?" Nothing could be more interesting than what Exley is about to utter.

He drops his chin and peers skeptically at Carson. "Carson, do you really want to hear about this?"

"Of course!"

"Do you?" he asks me.

I'm sitting on a desk, arms around my knees. I shrug. "Sure."

Exley claps his hands. "Great!" He leans forward conspiratorially. "I'm building a sand wall in my garden!"

"Wow!" Carson says.

Exley's face falls. "Thad's bored by this."

Carson glances at me. "No, he's not."

"Yes, he is. You're bored, Thad, aren't you?"

"A little," I admit.

Exley squints as if trying to see into my skull. "What is it that bores you?"

I make a face. "A 'project.' It sounds like building model airplanes or something."

Exley gnaws his mustache, nods thoughtfully. "It's sort of mediocre?"

"Yeah," I say, impressed despite myself. That's exactly what I mean. "It's mediocre."

Now Exley's eyes droop sensually. "But lo-ok," he says, drawing out the word. "What's not a project?"

I think for a moment. "Nothing, I guess."

Exley slaps his palm on his desk. "That's great!" He turns to Carson. "Do you *see*?"

Carson squints and nods. "He knows how to lose an argument?"

"Yes!"

I look from Carson to Exley. Now that I know what they consider an argument, I'll try harder next time.

———

As in Kansas, I cut classes and read in out-of-the-way corners of campus, albeit books recommended by Exley now—Carlos Castenada, Ram Dass, above all, Robert Pirsig's *Zen and the Art of Motorcycle Maintenance* ("Zen and the Art," we call it), which Exley is using to introduce Carson and me to philosophy.

Still, I wonder what I'm doing here. It's as if I died and drifted back without finding what I sought. Gradually, though, as the fluency of my surfing returns, I dream of rising again. In March

I enter a contest on a thin board Meta custom-shaped and sold to me for cost.

He watches from the boardwalk, nodding at the boy most likely to give me trouble as my heat trots down the beach. At Exley's suggestion, I've fasted for three days. My concentration has increased—that was the point—but I'm weak, and in the water a sort of paralysis steals over me. Watching my rival jounce his board up and down with pugnacious confidence—it seems to be some new technique for setting up the bottom turn—I can't decide whether I care too little or too much.

In any case, I lose.

———

In April, the phone rings. Hoping that it's Renee, the girl I've just begun dating, I close the book I'm reading and listen. Someone else has answered the upstairs extension, Carson or his mother.

The Colonel moved out not long after I arrived. Checking the surf one morning, Carson and I found him sleeping one off in his boxers, knees drawn up, like an ancient corpse in a glacier.

Mrs. Reynolds knocks softly. I call her by her first name now, Dolly.

"It's your mom, hon."

I walk down the hall and pick up the phone.

"I'm afraid I have some bad news," she says. Her voice is tiny, flat. "Pat's—"

"What?" She's speaking so softly.

"Pat's dead."

"Dead? How?"

I can't imagine what she'll say.

"He committed suicide, honey."

The picture of it won't form. "Are you sure?"

"He was depressed."

"About what?"

"He never got over being fired in Florida. But it was with him before that."

"I thought he lost his job because of not getting along with his boss."

"He didn't see it that way. He felt he'd failed."

There's no such thing as an accident.

———

After whispered discussion between Dolly and Carson, it's announced that he'll fly to Wichita with me. He's at his best in emergencies like this, steadfast and practical.

On the plane the next morning, I look at his face in profile, at a dazzlingly white cloud outside the window. The world, the value of things, their very substantiality—nothing is the same. It's as if a basis for how I gauge reality has been refuted.

In Wichita, the first buds have appeared on the trees. As we pull up to the house, Adam's in the street on a minibike, smiling. The tyrant is dead. He puts on a somber face when I catch his eye.

He's fourteen. In another fourteen years, he too will be dead by his own hand, hanged from a cord in the basement of a group house in D.C., tattoos on his face, among his few possessions a syringe. If he couldn't live in a tree, he didn't want to live at all.

In the house are people I don't know, laying out food, speaking in low voices. Mom is in the bedroom, grief-encircled. It's like a heavy smoke.

I sit beside her on the bed and hold her. Beneath the paisley housedress, her body seems melted, boneless. Pale Kansan sunlight leaks in through the drawn curtains.

———

"What happened?" Night has fallen. The house is quiet. We're alone in the bedroom again.

"Well, he was drinking a lot."

"Drinking?"

"It got worse after you left. That's when he started threatening to kill himself. One day he locked himself into the skateboard store and said he was going to do it there. And one night he got just crazy; he was drunk and started hitting me. I really thought he might kill me."

"God."

"I'm just glad you were in Florida.

"He wrote a letter apologizing." She gestures at papers scattered on the bed, among them a life-insurance policy he took out.

"It's here somewhere. Because I told him I would leave him. In the letter he said he had decided to live, that he would never risk losing me or Jason."

Someone knocks, peers around the door, a woman I vaguely recognize. "Can I get you anything?"

"No, I'm fine. Thanks."

The door closes.

"I thought we had made it through a rough patch." She looks at her hand on the bedspread.

"Then one night he went out with his drinking buddies. Anyway, he stayed out so late I finally just went to bed."

She looks around the room, shakes her head slowly. "And in the middle of the night, I woke up. I saw him come in," she points to the door, "and go back out. I had this terrible feeling. I thought he was going to kill Jason and Adam and me and then himself."

She grips my hand. "I called his name. And right then the phone rang—it was the state police. They'd found him in the car on the side of the road. He'd shot himself with a rifle."

I'm confused. "So you saw him after—his ghost?"

She squeezes my hand and nods.

———

The funeral is closed-casket. I don't approach it, nor do I hear the words of the eulogies.

I sit with Jason, hold his small hand. He's six, clear-faced and solemn in a suit and tie, the angelic image of Pat. What does he understand? That his father is gone.

———

Gusts of wind jounce the tree limbs outside the large kitchen window. She's sorting through documents in a strongbox, the grace of her movements, her beauty, enhanced by grief as if in compensation.

"I'll move back," I offer.

To my relief, but shame too, she shakes her head, smiles. "You have a girlfriend, a good teacher. I want you to finish school down there. I'll be fine."

"Think about it."

But I know I won't have to live in this Middle Earth again; that she's freed me once more.

———

As it has been for years, the Kon Tiki is the afternoon haunt of the Colonel and his cronies, their Cadillacs parked in the rear lot like weathered boats, two-tone roofs blistering, chrome specked with rust. But at night the crowd is now much younger, though often one of the daylight number lingers like a truculent afterimage, head fallen forward.

I'm at a table with Renee. She has luminous green eyes and a chipped front tooth, small hands with a child's tapered fingers. At school, her persona is that of an ERA feminist, ethical and "strong." For a time, the shadow of Pat's suicide fell tragi-romantically across us. Now I worry she's growing bored, or that I am. The high drama of cajoling her into having sex is also past. She has a part-time job as a secretary in an insurance agency; on her days off she watches soap operas and eats homemade pizza.

"What do you think of the Medicaid abortion ruling?"

In my pocket is a piece of paper with other topics for conversation. It's pathetic. I jot them down while reading *Time* magazine.

Renee shrugs and stirs her drink, brooding again, probably

about her father, an instructor at a military academy who spends his time at home stretched out on the couch, Budweiser in hand, TV on. He's insisting that she major in business at college next year. It's like a death sentence.

A clutch of surfers has taken up position along the bar, pros I recognize vaguely from the magazines—Australians, South Africans, their hair shining in the light of the kitsch Polynesian torches. There's a contest being held at Sebastian Inlet.

One of them keeps turning to survey the room with that Apollonian surf-star arrogance, as if in search of challenger or virgin. I can't remember having seen anyone quite this inflated and supercilious, though. It's mesmerizing. I'd like to break a chair across his head; at the same time he seems far away, on the other side of a gulf.

That's no longer you, I tell myself. I've been writing stories, poems. There's a gay student whose work is admired by Exley and the literary circle at school. He's written a poem about the white and black horses in Plato's *Phaedrus*. Reading it, I could see them, winged, pulling the soul charioteer in contrary directions.

It was to compete with him that I began a poem, but like a current the words swept me beyond sight of that origin, out into regions of their own.

———

I stand in the shore break, one hand on the deck of my board. The warm water reaches my waist. A few small fish, flat and clear, suddenly scatter, one of them brushing my wrist.

We've moved, Carson, his mother and I, to the fifth floor of an unsightly new condominium built on the beach in Indialantic. The view from Carson's bedroom is like a shimmering ocean mural. I feel it at my back.

The window in my room gives on the vast, Wagnerian sunsets. They make me uneasy now; so do the velvety dusks that swallow them up. Carson and I have begun to drift apart, it's hard to say why—something unspoken, a strain arisen from competing for Exley's favor.

As I push off from shore—the shore on which Pat no longer resides, even unto Kansas—I notice a hairline fracture up by the board's nose and wonder idly how it happened. Then I paddle through the gap between two peaks, gouts of spray spattering my back, land and all that goes with it falling away.

A few years from now, in 1981, I'll ask Carson to ship this board to Washington, so I can bring it with me on my first trip to Europe. I'm living with my father by then, self-consciously getting to know him again and studying literature at the university where he's been on the faculty all these years.

I carry the board through Victoria Station in a box, sending it ahead via Paris to Biarritz, whose point breaks and pine-studded cliffs I know from surf magazines. It's May. Every morning for two weeks I pick my way over the rocks and ride the cold waves. The rest of the time I write in a journal, read, practice the French Corinne has been teaching me.

I'm waiting for something, a sign that it's time to turn away from the glittering water and go inland, to Europe proper, the cities and museums. Finally, one morning, the board breaks in two along the old crack. Gazing at the pieces washing up and back on the dark sand, I feel more relief than grief: I'm free to go all the way ashore.

That future moment, like the crack, is already present in this one. But here and now the ocean is all I know, the waves rising darkly, the way they move, the way to ride them, the water on which the thin board floats.

Epilogue

The sun is setting behind Queens, behind Manhattan, lights in apartment windows coming on. The man and children are gone. I can barely make out my bag onshore. It's time to head back to the city, where things will be more or less as before.

Though I do have a board again. It hasn't changed into a pool cue or two-by-four or otherwise obeyed the sick logic of my dreams. I'll carry it to Cornelia Street and up the stairs to our apartment, show it to Juliana, then lean it against the wall in the hallway. It will be there until I bring it back, set it in the water and paddle out again.

I might, I suppose, carry it farther, to places like Barbados and Eleuthera, paradisiacal places I've done my best to forget about, but which are resurfacing now, as after a flood.

I might go as far as Hawaii itself. The idea causes me to draw breath sharply, as if the islands had appeared in the sky. Hawaii. Is it still possible?

I turn seaward to look for a wave. The last is often elusive; it's as if, like a lonely child, one too proud to say simply, "Don't go! I don't *want* you to go!," the ocean contrives indirect ways to prevent your leaving: lulls set in, or only below-average waves appear, and no one wants the last to be anything less than good.

Epilogue

Eventually it arrives, separating itself from the darkening water like a living thing. I catch it, stand, turn once, then lie down and ride the white water to shore.

I tuck the board under my arm, walk up the sand and, as ever, pause to look back at the ocean, whence I came.

Acknowledgments

T hanks first of all to my wife, Juliana Ellman, for her devotion and faith, priceless close readings of the manuscript and pitch-perfect suggestions, for lifting my spirits with surf videos and indulging my inevitable wish for "one more wave."

Thanks to my mother and father for their love and support, and to the Ellmans for theirs. Thanks to Henry Dunow, my agent, for his vision, heart and tenacity. Thanks to Elisabeth Schmitz of Grove/Atlantic for her gimlet editorial eye and nuanced shaping of the book's final form. Thanks to my readers Laurie Stone and James Marquand for their many fine suggestions. Thanks to Bruce Hainley for his friendship and belief in the project, and to Linda Darling and J. Anderson, surf buddy extraordinaire, for theirs. Thanks to Jason Burke for tending the flame of paradise. Thanks to Bob Nickas and Peter Halley of *Index,* and Sheila Glaser of *Travel & Leisure,* for nurturing embryonic versions of this book. And thanks to Pratt Institute for its support in the form of two Faculty Research Awards.